RESOLVED

RESOLVED

Debate Can Revolutionize Education and Help Save Our Democracy

ROBERT LITAN

BROOKINGS INSTITUTION PRESS

Washington, D.C.

Library of Congress Control Number: 2020943110
ISBN 9780815737872 (pbk : alk. paper)
ISBN 9780815737889 (ebook)

9 8 7 6 5 4 3 2 1

Typeset in Calluna

Composition by Elliott Beard

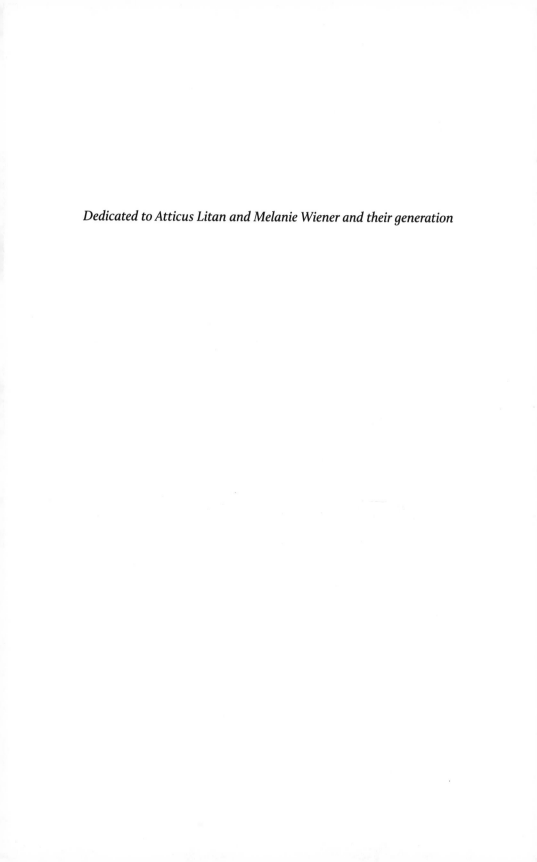

Dedicated to Atticus Litan and Melanie Wiener and their generation

Contents

Contents

Preface

Fiction authors are commonly advised to "write what they know." Nonfiction authors, especially those at think tanks like the Brookings Institution, are a bit different. They write about what they research, and through the course of their careers, they often change fields to mix things up. That pretty much sums up what I have tried to do during my research career, most of it affiliated with Brookings.

In recent years, I have concentrated my research on the influence and nature of economics itself. In 2014, I authored a book *The Trillion Dollar Economists*, about how economics and economists have had hugely influential, though until then not widely recognized, influence on business in America. As 2016 was beginning, I was planning to follow up that book with another about economics, but focused on how much the field has changed, specifically through the mushrooming use of randomized control trials (RCTs)—of the kinds use to test new drugs—in economics and social sciences generally, and how the use of such information is increasingly being viewed as important by policymakers. The appointment in 2016 of a Commission on Evidence-

Based Decision-Making, based on legislation authored by Senator Patty Murray (D-Washington) and then Speaker of the House Paul Ryan, one of whose chairs was my Brookings colleague Ron Haskins, seemed to make that book timely.

I had a change of heart about writing such a book after the 2016 election results, fearing there wouldn't be much of a market for a manuscript about evidence-based decisionmaking. Ironically, I was wrong about the market. Yale University Press (the intended publisher of the book I initially was going to write) published in 2018 an excellent book, *Randomistas*, on the history and utility of RCTs by noted economist and Australian politician Andrew Leigh. In the fall of 2019, three economists—Abhijit Banerjee, Esther Duflo, and Michael Kremer (with whom I had the privilege of working at Brookings two decades ago)—shared the Nobel Prize in Economics for their pioneering use of RCTs in testing various "micro-interventions" to reduce poverty.

In any event, by the time the Leigh book was available, I had mentally moved on, writing several essays for the Brookings website in 2017 and early 2018 about the fraying American political fabric, ways to help the middle class without reducing economic growth, and the worries but also the misconceptions about continued automation. All these essays were prompted by concerns I suspect bother most Americans, making them fearful or even angry. These are also the concerns I focused on after organizing and hearing comments at a conference held in June 2016 at Stanford's Institute for Economic Policy Research (SIEPR) to discuss an outline for the book I had initially intended to write. I am grateful to the Smith Richardson Foundation that generously provided the financial support for this working conference and to the foundation for the patience it displayed while I decided to write a very different book (this one), and to the many well-known economists who showed up to participate at the Stanford session.

One comment at that conference by one of my lifelong friends and mentors, Stanford emeritus professor Roger Noll, struck a special chord with me, however. He suggested that instead of writing a broadbased book—the kind Leigh had written—I should focus on one or two specific public policy challenges where the empirical revolution in economics was having a real impact. That explains why I wrote the Brookings essays on the growing incivility in public life and the seemingly intractable problem of growing income inequality, topics which, not surprisingly, are related to one another.

But I didn't yet have the desire or the "hook" to write another full book until, quite by accident, I read an article in April 2018 on my Twitter feed. The article was written by a journalist at the *Christian Science Monitor* who highlighted the surprising (to her) importance of competitive high school debate in my home state of Kansas.[1] The article caught my eye because a little more than 50 years ago, I, too, was a competitive high school debater in Kansas (who went on to debate a little more than two years at the college level before turning to my real intellectual passion, economics, full time). Also, as I explain in the first chapter, debate fundamentally changed my life, and I instinctively felt I had something more to say about the virtues of debate, potentially for others. I didn't realize the extent of those virtues at the outset, however—not until I began the research about to be described.

Before doing that, a remarkable coincidence is worth mention. Two months after the *Christian Science Monitor* article published, a high school team from Blue Valley Southwest in Johnson County, Kansas, part of the larger Kansas City metro area, won the national high school championship in "policy debate" that year. Also, in that same year, a team from Kansas University won the college policy debate championship (readers will learn about the multiple debate formats that have developed as alternatives to policy debate and the main reason why, in chapter 2). Even more remarkably, the following year, *two* Kansas teams from the same high school, Washburn Rural in Topeka, qualified for the championship round at the national high school tournament, only the second time that has happened in the history of the national tournament, making the second year in a row that a Kansas team won the national championship. Another Johnson County, Kansas, high school team made it to the semifinals of the 2019 tournament, as did a team from Kansas University in the college national tournament that year.

I digress (though with pride). The key for you, the reader, is that the article to which I refer somehow lit a lightbulb in my head, giving me the spark, the energy, and the enthusiasm it takes to write any book. Almost instantaneously, the article prompted the following thought experiment: "What if every high school student had debate training, and specifically the research, thinking, organizational, and speaking skills that debaters develop, and most important, the ability to take *both or multiple sides* of an issue in a public way before a real audience? Wouldn't students have more fun in school and learn more while they're there? Wouldn't students be better prepared for the workforce? Wouldn't our country and our democracy be in a better place?

My gut answers to all these questions was yes, and those answers, fully fleshed out, form the core of this book. But still, the structure of a book wasn't immediately apparent to me, nor was I sufficiently confident that it would have an audience. I needed, first, to get some feedback from the people I thought could give me some honest input—those with some debate or debate coaching experience themselves. So, I began emailing and talking to many such individuals. To a person, everyone also said yes to one or more of my questions.

These outreach efforts gave me the confirmation and enthusiasm I needed to make the two-year time investment of research and writing that it took to write this book. Thank goodness, I had a lot of help along the way. Michael Harris, the debate coach at Wichita East High School, and Scott Harris, the head coach at Kansas University, and his assistant coach Brett Bricker (a former national college debate champion), were all extremely useful sources in these early interviews, and highly encouraging about the project. Norman Ornstein, one of the nation's most prominent political scientists and a long-time scholar at the American Enterprise Institute, also helped me organize my thoughts at a very early stage, while giving me excellent advice and encouragement. He later kindly reviewed and helped improve the draft manuscript.

I also am deeply indebted to the many other people who took the time to talk with me, including:

AnneMarie Baines (former debater and debate coach, founder of "Practice Space")

Alex Berger (former champion high school and college debater, now a Hollywood screenwriter)

Bo Cutter (former high-ranking White House official during the Carter and Clinton administrations)

Jesus Caro (former debate coach at Marjorie Stoneman High School, Broward County, Florida)

Diana Carlin (former high school and college debater and debate coach and former professor of communications and Dean of the Graduate School at the University of Kansas)

Francesca Haass (the ex-debater daughter of my former Brookings and Council on Foreign Relations colleague Richard Haass)

Brian Hufford (ex-debater at Wichita State and now outstanding trial attorney in Baltimore)

Jeff Jarman (former national college debate champion and now the dean of the Elliott School of Communications and head debate coach at Wichita State University)

Alexa Kemper (former high school debater from Lee's Summit, Mo., who twice debated at the national high school championship tournament)

Megan Kowaleski (debate program coordinator, Success Academy schools, New York)

Linda Listrom (former executive director of the National Association of Urban Debate Leagues)

Joe Loveland (former champion debater at the high school and college levels, and successful litigator)

Annika Nordquist (a former high school debater and the daughter of a good friend and former Brookings colleague, D. J. Nordquist)

Gallo Pitel (a high school debater at Stuyvesant High School in New York, and Cutter's grandson)

Nicole Wanzer-Serrano (director of development, National Speech and Debate Association)

Cy Smith (former high school and college debater, and outstanding trial attorney in Baltimore)

Bill Thompson (debate coach, NSU School, South Florida)

Eric Tucker (former deputy director of the National Urban Debate League, and co-founder, with his wife Erin Mote, of the Brooklyn Labs school in New York city)

Dave Trigaux (executive director of Washington D.C. Urban Debate League and the Matthew Ornstein Summer Debate Camp)

Brian Wannamaker (former Kansas high school debater)

Stephanie Wu (former high school debater in Australia and college debater at the University of Pennsylvania)

Scott Wunn (executive director of the National Speech and Debate Association)

Early in my research, however, I realized I was talking only to people well versed in *competitive* debate, which at best engages 1 percent, most likely less, of all high school students. With the help of Todd Fine, a former national high school debate champion and son of Gary Fine, a sociologist at Northwestern, whose book *Golden Tongues* is the best academic treatment of high school debate I have seen, I was introduced to a small cadre of education pioneers. One of these was Les Lynn in Chicago, the founding director of the National Association of Urban Debate Leagues and the first to "debatify" (his term) the high school educational curriculum in the work he does with his current organization, Argument-Centered Education. Shortly thereafter, I stumbled across Mike Wasserman, executive director of the Boston Debate League [BDL]). Lynn and Wasserman, and the BDLs' experienced team of coaches, have been assisting schools and teachers in Chicago and Boston to use debate and argument-based instructional techniques throughout the high school curriculum, and even in pre-high school grades. You will learn much about Les, Mike, the BDL, and the schools they are assisting in chapter 3 of the book.

I cannot thank both Lynn and Wasserman enough for educating me about their work, and for also organizing my visits in the spring of 2019 to Chicago and Boston, respectively, to see in action the teachers they are mentoring. I want to thank each of these dedicated professionals and their students for opening my eyes—and through me, hopefully, yours—to their cutting-edge use of argument-based learning. At Proviso West High School outside Chicago, I want to thank these teachers for allowing me to observe their classes: Sherry Bates, Danielle English, Angda Goel, Adenike Natschke, and Stephen Ngo. In Boston, thanks go to BDL's experienced coaches, Sarah Mayper, Marisa Suescun, and Kim Willingham, and to these teachers: Melissa Graham at the Lilla G. Frederick Pilot Middle School and Patti Dennis, Doris Kane, Mike Nickerson, and Vanessa St. Leger at the Henderson School.

I previewed the broad outlines for the arguments in this book in a blog post I wrote for Brookings in September 2018 titled "A Counterintuitive Proposal for Improving Education and Healing America: Debate-Centered Instruction,"[2] which I draw on in various places, especially in chapter 1. I want to thank Jonathan Rauch, a coauthor from over twenty years ago and a close friend and Brookings colleague, for suggesting that I write that initial essay, both to get my thoughts "out there" for public view and to gain valuable feedback and information for possible readers of a future book. He was right on both counts. Numerous people, many of them former debaters, saw the essay and did precisely what Jonathan had forecasted: they gave me both positive and constructive feedback and made me aware of professionals around the country who were using debate-centered instruction in their educational systems. Indeed, this is how I met Mike Wasserman of the BDL and Scott Wunn and Nicole Wanzer-Serrano of the National Speech and Debate Association, who kindly promoted the Brookings essay through social media.

I am also grateful to *Atlantic* editor Jim Fallows, Jeff Finkle, president of the International Economic Development Council, and Frank Partnoy of Berkeley Law School (all former high school and college debaters, which I also didn't know until we talked), who strongly encouraged me at the beginning of this project to see it through. Likewise, I greatly appreciate the close editing of an earlier draft of this book by my law school classmate, and former high school and college debater, Don Sloan.

Likewise, I gained much from reconnecting with my long-time friend Ken Kay, who has been a leader in education reform from his home in Arizona since leaving his Washington, D.C. law practice about two decades ago. Ken founded EdLeaders21, since absorbed by Battelle for Kids, which helps superintendents around the country to stay on the cutting edge of education pedagogy. In addition to providing valuable advice that is relevant to the last chapter of the book, Ken introduced me to the remarkable book by Ten Dintersmith, *What School Could Be*, which I reference and draw on at several points in pages that follow. For those who agree with Dintersmith's emphasis that "project based learning" (PBL) is the best way to prepare students for the twenty-first century, consider this book a companion, for debate centered instruction has features akin to PBL while also offering the advantages of developing students' oral communications skills and furthering a mindset that will make them better workers and citizens when they reach adulthood.

I also want to give a big shout out to Megan Callaghan of Bard College, who furnished me with important facts about Bard's Prison Initiative, and the debate team inside prison it fosters, which readers will learn about in chapter 6, and to Lynn Novick, who created a documentary about these debaters, for introducing me to Megan.

As I wrote the book, I often thought of my debate partners in high school (Jan Hornberger Duffy, Gretchen Miller, and the late Marc Salle) and college (Brian Jones, Don Klawiter, and high school coach William Robinson). Without them, debate wouldn't have changed my life in the way I describe in the book, and I certainly wouldn't have had the faintest idea of why and how to write a book that draws on that experience. I hope they enjoy and maybe even agree with what follows.

I showed early drafts of this book to numerous people, and I thank every one of them, they know who they are, and the book would not be what it is without their help. I also thank each of the individuals who formally reviewed the book at the request of the Brookings Institution Press. Although readers won't know where and how, I assure you that the comments I received greatly improved what you are about to read.

I benefitted greatly from the advice of William Finan, director of the Brookings Institution Press, who enthusiastically took this project on, and the careful editing of Kathi Anderson.

Finally, I am grateful to my wife, Margaret, for encouraging me not only to undertake this project but in everything else I do (and not minding the workaholic tendencies that book writing brings out in me). She has never been intimidated by my debate experience, although she sometimes will jokingly suggest during a discussion, "You must have learned that in debate." To all future debaters, in competition or in classrooms, you will probably have similar experiences in your lives, which I hope will be one of many reasons you find debating to be such a valuable skill. And to those who don't have a formal debate background, I hope you will find what follows to be engaging and inspiring—enough so that you, too, can help revolutionize education and help save our democracy!

In early March 2020, mayors, governors, and ultimately President Donald Trump began enforcing strict social distancing measures in response to the COVID-19 pandemic, whose unprecedented economic consequences will be felt for at least a few years. My heart goes out to all who have lost loved ones during this awful episode in our history.

The pandemic forced the closure of schools throughout the United States, and led me to modify some of my recommendations for universal debate-centered instruction in at least high schools to take into account remote learning, which fortunately was available for most U.S. students during the crisis and may need to be used more regularly in the future, even without another pandemic. Paradoxically, many students may find it easier to express themselves orally in the comfort of their own homes—talking through a computer—than in front of their schoolmates in a typical classroom setting.

More experimentation with debate-centered instructional techniques in remote settings should be undertaken. Hence, the recommendations outlined here may be even more relevant and important than before the outbreak of the pandemic and the need to transition to remote learning.

RESOLVED

ONE

Improving Education and Healing America through Debate-Centered Education

An Introduction

> I think debating in high school and college is most valuable training whether for politics, the law, business or for service on community committees such as the PTA and the League of Women Voters . . . I wish we had a good deal more debating in our educational institutions than we do now.
>
> *President John F. Kennedy, August 1960[1]*

America is as divided politically and economically as it has been at any point in my lifetime, nearly seven decades long, a period that spans the divisive and tumultuous years of the Vietnam War and, later, Watergate. People are sorting themselves, in their work and at home, into "blue" and "red" bubbles to an unprecedented degree, and increasingly are living in very different worlds, choosing their news sources and friends and splitting their families along political lines.[2] Widening income inequality (especially manifest in the wide disparities of who has suffered the most during the economic contraction triggered by the COVID-19 pandemic in 2020), the economic division between rapidly growing blue regions of the country and less rapidly growing areas, or even shrinking red regions,[3] coupled with the receding American Dream for too many, all surely have made matters worse.

We are now more than just polarized and are growing more so at a faster rate than other industrialized countries.[4] We are becoming tribal, where whatever you may say or write is viewed by others entirely according to which side of the political divide you fall. Former Secretary of Defense and highly decorated Marine general James Mattis put it well when he wrote these words in August 2019: "We are dividing into hostile tribes cheering against each other, fueled by emotion and a mutual disdain that jeopardizes our future, instead of rediscovering our common ground and finding solutions."[5]

At no time in recent history has this tribal conflict been more on display, and the political rancor more in evidence, than during the impeachment of President Donald Trump. As this book went to market, the country headed into unchartered territory with an impeached but not convicted president campaigning for reelection only several months into the nation's experience of its second-greatest pandemic and one of its worst recessions in history. It remains to be seen whether the only silver linings in this horrible episode—the extraordinary coming together of people online and the support for medical professionals and millions of lower-paid "essential workers" who fought the pandemic on its front lines and kept the economy from totally collapsing—will begin to heal the country's deep political divisions, or whether those divisions will grow deeper.

Political leaders, academic and think tank scholars, journalists, and pundits across the political spectrum have suggested several ways to do what General Mattis urged before the pandemic crisis to bridge the differences between us. Some options have to do with changing the institutions of government to encourage more political moderation and compromise: finding ways to reverse and prevent gerrymandering (such as using independent commissions to draw district lines); changing the mechanics of voting (such as a nonpartisan primary system that picks the top two candidates for each elected office, regardless of party, to run in the general election, or choosing the winner based on voters' rank order preferences); or eliminating the electoral college, if not by constitutional amendment then by enough states passing legislation declaring the presidential victor in each state as the one receiving a majority of the national vote, which would accomplish the same objective.

Another very different idea for helping bridge our political divisions is to require young people, after high school or college, to devote at least a year to national service, either military or civilian.[6] In addition to fixing some of America's problems, national service would mix Americans of all backgrounds at a highly impressionable age, reducing stereotyping, building empathy, and restoring some sense of national cohesion and purpose.

This book advances a very different, perhaps counterintuitive, prescription: incorporate debate or evidence-based argumentation in school as early as the late elementary grades, clearly in high school, and even in college. Debate-centered education, as I call it (it has other names, as you will learn) would excite students about learning, thereby enhancing their engagement and performance. In addition, there are good reasons for believing it also would enhance their earnings prospects throughout their working lives while helping to heal our political and economic rifts.

Debating has deep historical roots. Its use in education, resolving legal disputes, and by deliberative bodies of all sorts hearkens back to ancient Greece and Rome, and to famous philosophers such as Aristotle and Socrates. Civil discourse through debate among candidates for political office, and among citizens, also has long been a characteristic of effective democracy.

Why not, then, greatly expand debate participation beyond the world of "competitive debating," which for decades has been limited to a small fraction of the U.S. high school student population? It seems like an easy question to answer in the affirmative. But the fact is that debate as an instructional device is rarely used in school classrooms. I have written this book to persuade school leaders, policymakers, and the wider public why this should change.

I know I can't wave a magic wand and make the changes I recommend happen all at once. At best, debate-centered instruction (DCI) will take decades to fully penetrate the education system, while moving it into the entire electorate will take even longer. Skeptics who are persuaded by the case I am about to make will correctly point out that we do not have the luxury of time. We need to heal our nation much sooner, for all kinds of reasons. I agree with that; if you do, too, then I hope you can be in the vanguard that brings about the reform outlined here much more quickly. However rapidly change comes, we must start somewhere and some time. Why not now?

The Virtues of Debate: A Preview

My case begins by recognizing and then building on the virtues of competitive debating, whose major features are outlined in the next chapter. Until you get there, all you need to know is that competitive debating, even with some of the changes over the years that I criticize in later portions of the book and which a few critics claim would harm our national political discourse if widely adopted, is very much the antithesis of the partisan and uncivil shouting matches we see daily on cable TV or in congressional floor speeches. Debating in school develops a much different and much more important set of skills: research; thinking logically and critically and doing it on your feet; listening carefully to others; backing up arguments with evidence (not fake news!); working collaboratively with partners; speaking persuasively in a civil fashion; and perhaps most important, being able to argue both (in some cases more) sides of nearly any issue or subject. Understanding how to identify and articulate the merits and drawbacks of multiple sides of almost any subject or issue is important in all phases of life and is key to a healthy democracy.

Although it has had problems counting votes in elections, one county in Florida, Broward, is a national leader in recognizing the educational power of having its students participate in some form of debating activity, and proudly touts the improvements in educational performance that have resulted.[7] Since 2013, all high schools, middle schools, and even elementary schools beginning with 4th grade in the county have been required to offer speech and debate classes. After getting off to a slow start, this "Broward Initiative" is now thriving, with over 12,000 students currently participating. It is not surprising, therefore, that two of the leaders of the national movement for gun control who emerged after the mass shooting at Marjorie Stoneman High School in Parkland, Florida, centered in Broward County, in February 2018, David Hogg and Jacklyn Corin, debated competitively.[8] Several other students from the school had been preparing for debates over gun control before the tragic shooting took place.

Hundreds of thousands of former competitive debaters know the value of debate from their own experiences. Many successful politicians, actors, and business leaders were once debaters. Look through the sample list provided at the end of this chapter. Some of the names there may surprise you.

Over two decades ago, a cadre of educators believed that competitive debating—through its training in research, thinking, and speaking—would be especially valuable for minority students, who often come from low income families and attend school in urban school districts. In the late 1990s, these educators put this idea into practice by forming city-wide "urban debate leagues," initially in Atlanta, and shortly thereafter in Baltimore, Chicago, and New York. With early major financial support from the Open Society Institute (OSI), the National Association for Urban Debate Leagues (NAUDL) was formed in 2000 as a national organization to help these city-specific debate leagues in the United States. The idea borrowed from similar efforts by OSI to spur competitive debate programs in high schools and colleges in Asia and Eastern Europe as a way of inculcating free speech and democratic values in those parts of the world. The NAUDL, and its over twenty debate leagues around the country, is still going strong, even without OSI's support, roughly twenty years later. Similar efforts aimed at enhancing the education of minority students on a state-wide basis can be found in some states, such as the Speak First program in Alabama.[9]

But the adult success of former debaters does not necessarily prove that their participation in competitive debate was primarily or even partially responsible for that success. Former debaters may have become accomplished as they aged because they have the traits that would have made them successful anyhow and only incidentally participated in debate in their formative years because they were and still are naturally good speakers and students. Chapter 2 reviews some studies that take account of this possible "self-selection" bias and shows through one rigorous statistical method that, in fact, competitive debate has made a positive difference among minority debaters, especially girls.

That the limited evidence of the value of competitive debate is positive should not be surprising. Even the most naturally gifted people can and do benefit from formal instruction in any activity, especially when combined with practice and hard work. Just ask Michael Jordan, Lebron James, or Patrick Mahomes, or any other highly successful athlete, entertainer, or teacher. Indeed, what is true for successful adults is also true for students, as the pioneering research of psychologist Angela Duckworth shows. "Grit," as she calls it, is as or potentially more important for success in school and later in life as innate talent. Using the principles of debate more broadly in all classroom settings can be a powerful way of engaging students in the fun of learning, thereby encouraging them to stick with education—precisely the trait of grit that Duckworth has documented to be so important in education and in life.

In any event, in my own case, selection bias clearly wasn't an issue. Until the age of fifteen, I had a severe stutter, and my mother, on the suggestion of a friend, had to more than twist my arm to persuade me to enroll in a speech and debate class in my sophomore year in high school. Thank goodness she did, because competitive debate cured the speech impediment that, up to that point, had made me reluctant to speak up in class and which years of formal speech therapy was unable to fix. It also taught me the research and thinking habits that gave me the confidence to succeed in school and have a successful professional career thereafter. In interviews conducted for this book, I have listened to similar and even more compelling stories of how debate transformed the lives of people starting out in life with much greater disadvantages than me.

One such example is Eric Tucker, who grew up in Iowa in a low-income household with multiple learning issues and self-admitted behavioral issues. He says he was enticed into competitive debate in middle and high school by the prospect of traveling and hanging out with cool kids. Debate gave Eric a purpose in life, helping overcome his learning difficulties (which clearly were greater than my own) to gain an Ivy League education and then a Ph.D. in social science at Oxford, after which he joined, to help run, the National Association of Urban Debate Leagues. Afterward, Tucker and his wife Erin Mote founded the Brooklyn Labs charter school, which, at this writing, has over 800 students, almost all minorities, many with learning disabilities (like those Tucker overcame), and currently teaches students from the 6th through the 10th grade.[10]

That so many educators and students have participated in various forms of competitive debate over multiple decades suggests that, at the very least, there must be some value added to the activity beyond self-selection—though I admit more rigorous evaluations of the kinds I will soon describe are necessary. But why should the skills that competitive debate teaches to participants be limited to just them? Why shouldn't all students, not just the less than 1 percent who debate competitively, have an opportunity to acquire such skills?

Debate-Centered Instruction in Action

In fact, as you will learn in chapter 3, several educators have been hard at work on a little-noticed effort to incorporate debate- or argument-centered instructional techniques into other parts of the high school (and lower school) curriculum and classes. A pioneer of this kind of learning, Les Lynn, the founding executive director of the NAUDL, calls this "debatifying" the curriculum. Lynn has developed a set of materials, featured on his website, to enable teachers to do precisely this across a wide range of subjects, including science, where one wouldn't think debate instructional techniques would be useful or appropriate.[11]

Similarly, the Boston Debate League (BDL) has been assisting over a dozen Boston-area schools in a similar way since 2013. Lynn's and the BDL's activities implement, in multiple innovative ways, "debate across the curriculum," a pedagogical approach that has been advocated in a theoretical way over several decades by multiple researchers from different academic backgrounds,[12] which Lynn, the BDL, and the teachers they mentor have put into practice.

Well before any of these academic articles were written or Lynn and the BDL's current leader Mike Wasserman became active, one middle school teacher—in Dodge City, Kansas, in the 1980s—experimented with the notion that debate techniques could be useful in nonspeech classroom settings. Former debater and current trial lawyer Brian Hufford recounted to me that his teacher in a "citizenship class" in 9th grade had the students argue both sides of different propositions, such as what policy stance the United States should take vis-à-vis the Soviet Union.[13] He told me that this exercise taught him to look at issues from both perspectives—one of the most important lessons rules-based debating imparts to all students. Hufford's experience also enticed him to become a competitive debater in high school, which, in turn, led to a full scholarship to debate in college and put him on his way toward his outstanding legal career.

As multiple researchers have written, and as Lynn, Wasserman, and the teachers they have coached have told me—and common sense is likely to tell you—students are much more likely to remember what they research and debate than when some or even much of the material is delivered to them by "the sage on the stage" in lecture format that they then regurgitate on an exam. It is often said that the best way to learn something is to teach. Debate-centered education takes this adage up a notch, requiring students not only to teach but also to anticipate and counter questions and opposing arguments, activities that teacher-delivered lectures do not promote.

British educator Lucy Crehan, whose *Cleverlands* provides a comprehensive survey of why school systems in other countries are outperforming those in the United States, observes that the "motivation of students plays a huge part in whether they succeed . . ."[14] Having to prepare for and participate in a debate in class, perhaps first in small groups and later before the entire class, should be an ideal way to motivate students of all ages, but especially those in middle and high school, when students hit the first stage in life where they want to express themselves as individuals separate from their parents. Structured debate formats make that possible, making learning enjoyable and worth pursuing.

I am not claiming that DCI is the only way to do this. As Ted Dintersmith makes clear in his compelling and pathbreaking book *What Schools Could Be*, multiple educational innovation efforts are underway across the country, primarily in conventional public schools, to engage students in the joy of learning, organized around solving society's problems. Many of these efforts are described under the umbrella of project-based learning (PBL).[15] Tom Vander Ark, former director of education grantmaking at the Bill & Melinda Gates Foundation and deputy secretary of the U.S. Department of Education, has compiled an even broader list of innovative instructional techniques being used by both conventional and charter public high schools throughout the country.[16]

Dintersmith also makes a compelling case in his book not only for PBL but against the use of standardized test scores to measure student and teacher performance. Whether or not you are convinced of his arguments, the education establishment is not likely to abandon test scores any time soon as a measurement tool, and so I make the case that DCI can improve *both* test scores and interest in learning (which otherwise is deterred by a single focus on test score improvement) as well as workplace skills and civic life. One can be an advocate for PBL *and* DCI, viewing DCI as a type of ongoing project. The closing chapter of the book suggests that a linkage of DCI and PBL as part of a broader "education innovation" campaign could be the best way to expand the implementation of both ideas.

I cannot overemphasize the importance of making debate a central part of learning during the school day and not just expanding students' participation either in competitive debate or some variation of it as an extracurricular activity. Education researchers and practitioners Jal

Mehta and Sarah Fine have reported the huge problem of boredom in high schools all across America—only 32 percent of students reported being "engaged" in school, according to a Gallup poll taken in 2015—and have suggested that competitive debate, along with theater and sports, *after school* can help address the problem by giving students "much more agency, responsibility and choice."[17] DCI would do the same thing for all students, *in all their classrooms, potentially throughout every school day.*

One of the school leaders Mehta and Fine interviewed highlights another problem endemic to all K-12 education, but especially at the high school level: "Most schools and classrooms are set up in ways that trigger adolescents to resist. What we need to do is to trigger their instinct to *contribute*"[18] (emphasis added). By directly involving students in their own learning and in teaching others, and by enabling them to express themselves in a civil and constructive way in front of their peers, DCI directly answers this challenge.

DCI also should be attractive to teachers, many of whom may be initially skeptical of the idea. It reduces the number of lectures teachers must give and turns them more into mentors. I suspect many teachers would enjoy this mentorship function as much as, if not more than, delivering lectures, especially if they get better educational results. Moreover, DCI does not require all teachers to be superstars. The techniques of teaching through debate are replicable, scalable, and capable of being implemented well, even mastered, by all teachers who believe in it and want to make it work.

There Is Enough Evidence to Warrant Further Experimentation with DCI

DCI does not require all students take an introductory course in forensics and debate to prepare themselves for debates in the classroom. With a limited amount of upfront training, and some coaching or mentoring throughout the school year, any teacher instructing any subject can transform her classes, using the same curriculum she is already teaching, into debate-enhanced centers of excellence. The modest cost for doing all this can and should come out of existing professional development budgets that are now used to fund a variety of professional development programs for teachers. Although there may be some resistance to reallocating a limited portion of such existing budgets to DCI, as more teachers learn of the advantages to students and to them of DCI, such resistance should wane.

Ideally, the education philanthropic community, which historically has shown great interest and financial support for education reform, will turn its attention to this agenda: supporting more research into, development of, and experimentation with ways to introduce debate-centered instructional techniques into elementary, middle, and high school classes; in developing curricula or materials that can be easily adapted by teachers so that each doesn't have to reinvent the wheel; launching state-based summer institutes for training public school teachers (with scholarships) in debate-centered techniques; and funding rigorous evaluations not only to test the validity of the concept but to provide teachers with scientifically grounded feedback about how to improve such instruction.

Perhaps philanthropists, working with school districts, and researchers will be motivated by this book to launch one or more randomized control trials (RCTs)—long the standard in testing the efficacy and safety of new pharmaceuticals and more recently used for assessing various educational reform ideas—of DCI, with performance measures not limited to educational performance and teacher satisfaction during a few years but broadened and extended for a sufficient length of time to measure the longer-term workforce and civic benefits of this instructional technique. However, even in the best of circumstances, developing, funding, and assessing those studies and their results may be a decade away or more. Can we afford to wait?

I believe not, and I will show in the course of this book that a strong presumptive case already exists for all these benefits, enough so that much experimentation and refinement of DCI is warranted *now*.

Indeed, my intention is to convince you through a combination of logic and evidence that when those definitive studies are finally completed, they will confirm the propositions advanced here, or at the very least point the way to how DCI can be refined to achieve the multiple benefits I assert for it throughout this book.

More specifically, there is presumptive evidence that much more widespread adoption of DCI would equip many more workers than otherwise would be the case to have the communications, critical thinking, and research skills that employers say they want. It would make workers and our entire economy more productive, which would translate to higher and potentially more evenly distributed and higher wages. Furthermore, if all Americans had the skills that debate imparts, many more of us would be more open-minded and, thus, the voting public eventually would be less—I believe much less—politically divided.

In this age of information silos on the internet and on television, the last claim may strike some readers as hopelessly idealistic. But bear with me; in chapter 5, I support this claim in more detail.

For now, it should be sufficient to note that our Founding Fathers recognized that reasoned, fact-based debate is essential for any democracy to function. It directly follows, therefore, that a citizenry equipped with the skills debaters must master should improve political discourse, the understanding of essential government activities, and thus the functioning of government itself.

To be sure, there is plenty of evidence from past U.S. presidential elections backing historian Yuval Harari's claim that many, perhaps even most, voters act on their feelings or emotions toward candidates or parties rather than using rational thought. [19] *Wall Street Journal* columnist Peggy Noonan has called this the "magic pony" syndrome, describing a series of recent presidents as magic ponies who lacked substantial executive experience but, nonetheless, were elected, in large part, as she sees it, because enough voters were sufficiently dissatisfied with the status quo to believe that only a new magic pony would solve their problems. [20] While Harari and perhaps many others would question whether voters will heed Noonan's plea to give greater weight to candidates' past relevant experience and deep knowledge—in other words, more weight to reason—the merits of her plea are hard to dispute. Even Harari himself demonstrates that the many challenges facing future leaders in this country and in others are extraordinarily complex and demand reasoned-based leadership. But for voters to realize and act on this insight, they must themselves be better trained in exercising reason above emotion.

Debate training can help do this, by ensuring that the next and future generations of young people have experience and training in arguing *both or multiple sides* of issues so that, by the time they reach adulthood, they will vote for and demand leaders who have these same qualities. DCI teaches through active student participation in learning that many, if not most, problems in life do not have simplistic solutions. Knowing this in high school makes it more likely that, as voting adults, students will be skeptical of those who promise them. Debate training also teaches that compromise is not a dirty word but something that is necessary for deliberative democratic government to work.

Properly run debates also have the virtue of separating ideas from the identities of those who offer them, while teaching participants to avoid putting labels—conservative or liberal, democratic or republican—on ideas, which should be considered on their merits rather than as markers of identity. This runs counter to the prevailing tribal tendencies in the voting public, as well as among elected officials or those running for office who seek to reinforce partisan divisions. But if Americans are ever to have a chance at tackling the many stiff challenges our society now faces—doing a better job of assuring that all benefit from economic growth, addressing climate change, reducing the large and growing structural federal budget deficit, and establishing a broadly acceptable compromise on immigration policy, among many other issues—governments must be led by those dedicated to solving problems rather than posturing politically for the next election.

Of course, substantive policy changes that address people's real fears that economic changes could leave them out in the cold would also clearly help. I and others have written essays or books offering sensible ways to help Americans adjust better to continued changes and to broaden the benefits of future growth. Some of those ideas are summarized later in this book, especially in chapter 5. But sensible ideas will be implemented only if voters rationally weigh them and then vote for representatives who support them. DCI can help bring this about.

If I am right about the educational and civic virtues of a debate-centered education, why shouldn't all voters, who are already adults, be trained in these techniques? In an ideal world, they would be. In the real world, however, it is unrealistic to expect an already highly polarized electorate to embrace such a broad educational reform for themselves, although one organization, Better Angels, discussed at the end of chapter 4, is trying to do something close to that. But it is not too early for a new generation to be exposed to and trained in debate-based thinking and learning. As they are, by osmosis, the benefits of such training should seep into the minds of some of their parents, in off-hand conversations or at the dinner table when topics like "What did you do or learn at school today?" are routinely discussed.

Some might say that the demise of civility in our political discourse, and even in many of our personal relationships, is irreversible. Or that too many parents will oppose education that purposefully teaches students to be open-minded, forgetting that this is precisely what education is supposed to foster. I do not believe that will happen, though. Most parents who see their children excelling and being excited about learning, especially if they see improvements in educational outcomes (grades and test scores today, hopefully better measures of educational attainment in the future) that I believe debate-centered education can and will deliver, will be pleased with these outcomes and will not resist them. Indeed, beyond the specific skills that DCI imparts, including the ability and willingness to see both (or multiple) sides of most issues, DCI makes learning exciting and fun. How many parents will be opposed to that?

I do not urge that DCI be adopted in a one-size-fits-all fashion imposed by the federal government, which is politically impossible in any event and inconsistent with local control of education in America, which has deep historical roots, but rather on a voluntary basis from the local level up. That may make the technique slower to penetrate the educational system—even assuming the formal evaluations prove to be positive, as I fully expect—but it also fits with the need for experimenting with and refining the idea, which may have to be tailored to benefit different student populations in different ways.

One major advantage of concentrating on improving instructional techniques is that they can improve all public schools without pitting advocates and opponents of public charter schools against each other. Shortly after the mid-term elections in 2018, *Wall Street Journal* columnist Jason Riley posted an op-ed declaring that the "blue wave may wash education reform away," referring to the growing opposition within the Democratic party to school choice, principally charter schools.[21] Whether or not this assessment proves true or lasting, it is a mistake in my view to equate education reform solely with parental or student choice, even for successful public charter schools. Pedagogical reform infused by debate or argument-centered education could be even more important than what kind of schools students attend, if the goal is, as it should be, to improve educational outcomes for *all students* in all types of public schools—conventional and charter—and especially for students from disadvantaged backgrounds who face steeper challenges than peers from higher income families and neighborhoods.

Getting from Here to There

Notwithstanding the clear educational, workplace, and civic benefits of DCI, persuading local school boards, principals, and even many teachers to embrace it will not be easy. Most school systems around the country face stiff fiscal challenges, and although the cost of the proposed reforms recommended here would be a wash if funded by reallocating existing teacher professional development monies, doing that may also be politically problematic, at least for a while. In addition, school boards, principals, and teachers are constantly being pitched all kinds of pedagogical reforms, and as a result there is understandable reform fatigue that works against widespread adoption of DCI techniques. That is why there is a need for the studies called for here. If they demonstrate the educational benefits of DCI, this would provide an important impetus for wider adoption.

I am also fully aware of how difficult change can be to accomplish, especially when good ideas are introduced from outside the "club" of existing practitioners. It took well over a hundred years for doctors and hospitals to give priority to hand washing as a way of preventing the spread of infections, a simple idea whose power was discovered in the nineteenth century by Joseph Lister. Or, in a completely different arena, it took a while—but at least a shorter period than hand washing in the medical context—for sports executives, managers, and coaches to embrace the power of statistics or "analytics" pioneered by Bill James in baseball and popularized by Michael Lewis in his best-selling book *Moneyball.* The baseball establishment is embracing the more recent efforts by innovators on the fringes of professional baseball to combine insights from physics and statistics to improve player performance with even greater speed.[22] I am hopeful, as an outsider to the educational establishment, that the faster dissemination of good ideas witnessed in sports will be replicated in education with the rapid and widespread adoption of DCI.

In the meantime, the fact that there are well over a million adults who have benefited from competitive debate in school should provide a natural constituency for change and activism to support a much larger role for debate in education. Former debaters know its pedagogical value and are ideal ambassadors to the education community to urge much wider use of debate techniques in all classrooms. Indeed, many elected officials at all levels of government—though, admittedly, not necessarily at the school board level—were former competitive debaters in high school, and perhaps in college, and for them urging DCI should be like pushing on an open door.

To be clear, I do not claim that requiring debate and introducing debate-centered education in nondebate courses will completely solve both the political and economic problems of the country, or even most of the challenges confronting K–12 education. Former Education Secretary Arne Duncan makes a powerful case in his book *How Schools Work* that major increases in teacher pay, coupled with true accountability, and multiple measures for reducing gun violence in schools (not just reasonable gun control measures), stand at the top of any "to do" list to improve American education, especially in its inner-city schools.[23] The argument here, rather, is more modest: that much wider participation in debate and the introduction of DCI techniques clearly belong on education reform, workforce improvement, and civic health agendas, ideally at or near the top of the list.

The logic supporting the expansion of DCI is compelling. I am confident that rigorous evaluation will confirm the logic or, at the very least, shape the ways in which American students are taught to search out and understand multiple sides of the issues they confront in their personal and political lives. The future health of our society and our economy may depend on it.

APPENDIX 1-A

Sample List of Former Debaters

Samuel Alito	Supreme Court Justice
Steve Bannon	Political strategist
James Belushi	Actor
John Belushi	Actor
Stephen Breyer	Supreme Court Justice
Bill Clinton	President
Hillary Clinton	Senator, secretary of state, presidential candidate
Calvin Coolidge	President
William G. Crow	Former chairman of the Joint Chiefs of Staff; U.S. military

Ted Cruz	Senator
Bo Cutter	White House official during Clinton years; private sector financier
James Fallows	Journalist and television personality
Dan Glickman	Congressmen, agriculture secretary; former head of the Motion Picture Association of America
Austan Goolsbee	Former chair, Council of Economic Advisers
Kamala Harris	Senator
Glenn Hubbard	Former chair, Council of Economic Advisers; dean, Columbia Business School
Lee Iacocca	Legendary corporate CEO
Richard Nixon	President
Frank Partnoy	Popular nonfiction author; law professor
Jane Pauley	Television journalist
Norman Pearlstine	Journalism executive
Jonathan Rauch	Journalist; prolific author
Franklin Roosevelt	President
Karl Rove	Political strategist
Robert Rubin	Financier; treasury secretary
Carl Schramm	Foundation president; entrepreneur
Heidi Schreck	Broadway star; playwright
John Sexton	College president
Lawrence Summers	Treasury secretary; president of Harvard
Margaret Thatcher	Former prime minister, United Kingdom
Lawrence Tribe	Constitutional lawyer
Malcom X	African American leader; activist
Elizabeth Warren	Senator and presidential candidate

Source: National Speech and Debate Association website: www.speechand
debate.org/alumni/?utm_source=newsletter&utm_medium=email&utm_
content=Alumni%2520page&utm_campaign=Family%252BNewlsetter%252
B20181220 and the author's own research.

Competitive Debate as a Model for Education Reform

Virtues and Limits

Although time has blended the memories of my debate rounds in multiple tournaments over the course of a little more than five years—counting both high school and a bit more than two years of college—I still remember anxiety bordering on fear before each preliminary round, especially if we made it to elimination rounds, as well as the thrill of placing in or winning some tournaments. These words from Vera Petrovic, then a senior at Lawrence High School in Lawrence, Kansas, who as a junior was voted the top speaker in one of the debate categories at the national high school championship in 2018, described my own experience many years ago and should resonate with anyone who has debated competitively: "An activity like debate can give [you] so many special skills for the rest of your life. But it can also make you feel incredibly doubtful sometimes, because you are going intellectually head to head with somebody. That can make you feel extremely insecure about your intellect or ability. I think everyone deals with that."[1]

When I debated competitively, there was only one format for doing so, what for some time has been called "policy debate," or "PD" for short. There are strict rules about how PD is structured, although debate strategies have evolved considerably over time to the point where someone my age who debated competitively would barely recognize the activity that once consumed us.

The substantive part of this book begins in this chapter, which describes, primarily for nondebaters but also for former debaters who may not realize how much the activity that once played an important part of their formative years has changed over the past several decades, how policy debate is structured, how and why it has changed, and how multiple other forms of debating have since arisen largely in response or as a reaction to those changes. This will provide context for the discussion and for my recommendation of putting *some form of debate* or structured research and argumentation into many more classrooms, primarily in high school but also in middle school and even college. This recommendation is made because the same set of skills that competitive debaters learn—which greatly benefit students not only in school but throughout their lives—can and should be taught much more widely. For this reason, it is useful, if not essential, to understand what competitive debaters do and the rules under which they operate, because those rules have broad application.

This is true notwithstanding some of the changes in competitive debate that clearly do *not* belong in the classroom, for reasons you will understand by the end of this chapter. While I understand and to a certain extent defend the reasons for those changes in debating formats and strategies, I am not totally persuaded they are all a net positive, even in the world of competitive debating. I will explain why, even though I do not anticipate that my critiques, which have been echoed by others, will change competitive debating any time soon. Debate coaches, mostly former debaters themselves, learn a certain style, and they teach it to their students, some of whom perpetuate it when they become coaches. In the interest of full transparency, readers should understand my own perspective toward what has happened in the competitive debating world before weighing my arguments about the need for more fundamental pedagogical reform in education based on aspects of competitive debate.

Policy Debate: Its Origins and Main Features

Policy debate has its roots in political debates, whether in the legislature or for various elected offices, such as the presidency. Some of the best-known formal debates were those between Stephen Douglas and Abraham Lincoln during their 1858 senate campaign in Illinois. Political debates at the presidential level first occurred during the 1960 presidential campaign, with the famous television debate between John F. Kennedy and Richard Nixon. Televised presidential debates became routine after the 1976 campaign when Jimmy Carter debated Gerald Ford.

Formal "public policy" debate—long the core debating format—began in the late 1900s at the college level but did not take off in high schools until after World War I, with the formation of the National Forensics League (the name was changed in 2014 to the National Speech and Debate Association, NSDA), based at Ripon College. Ripon held the first national high school tournament in 1931 with forty-nine schools. By the middle of the Depression, over 400 schools had debate tournaments. High school debating took a hiatus during World War II, but since then has grown, with some ups and downs, over the past several decades. Today, approximately 50,000 students in the United States participate each year in policy debate competitively.[2]

Policy debates basically have a single format. The NSDA for high school and a corresponding association for college debate choose a single debate topic in the form of a resolution—which typically asks whether the federal government should undertake some action. The NSDA has a committee, composed of high school debate coaches from around the country, that chooses the annual topic, which rotates between a domestic and foreign policy topic from year to year. The committee tries to pick topics that are both broad enough to allow for teams to present or "run" multiple kinds of "cases"—plans for implementing the resolution and justifications for it—and yet narrow enough to focus the debates and tournaments formed around them.

Policy debate teams consist of two people on each side, one taking the affirmative in support of the resolution or the proposed action, and the other taking the negative side. The initial "constructive" presentations are made in eight-minute slots, with four cross-examinations lasting three minutes each, and rebuttals, four minutes for each of the four speakers (the constructive and rebuttal periods are ten minutes and five minutes respectively when cross-examination is not part of the format, infrequent these days but common when I debated in both high school and college).

All policy debates begin with a "first affirmative" constructive presentation, which is a "canned" speech outlining the justification or the "need" for the resolution, and frequently it is memorized. That team's best orator typically is chosen to be the first affirmative speaker, although the first affirmative must also deliver the first rebuttal, which entails very different skills: responding to a range of critiques by both negative speakers, but especially the second negative, who critiques the affirmative's plan or defends the negative's counterplan, if the negative team takes that approach.

Debaters in all formats participate in tournaments involving multiple schools, which in some cases for larger tournaments can easily exceed 100 or even 200 teams. Tournaments typically have six or more "preliminary rounds," each with a winning and a losing team. Each participating team will take the affirmative and negative positions—both sides—an equal number of times during these preliminary rounds, which typically take place on a Friday afternoon and Saturday morning. In addition to deciding a winner, the judge must award "speaker points," on a sliding scale from 1 to 10 or from 1 to 30, to individual team members for their persuasiveness, speaking ability, and overall presentation. The top eight, sixteen, or thirty-two teams with the best preliminary records—the number scaled to the size of the tournament, and with total speaker points often breaking ties—advance to the elimination or championship rounds. This process winnows the field down to the top two teams debating for the overall tournament championship. The elimination rounds generally run late into Saturday afternoon or even nighttime, by which time virtually all the participating teams will have left the tournament.

At the high school level, although all the forms of debate are conducted under the auspices and rules of the NSDA, tournaments are convened separately at the state and "national circuit" levels. Different states have different rules on how long the debate season for public school debaters can last—some states allow it only for the first semester; others allow it throughout the school year—and how many tournaments specific teams from a school can attend apart from the district, regional, and state tournaments. Catholic schools have long maintained their own debate league and tournaments but use the same topic chosen by the NSDA. Over time, Catholic school tournaments have been opened to public and other private school teams as well.

Over the past several decades, a separate set of national circuit tournaments have developed that attract certain high school teams— from schools with long debate traditions and substantial budgets, and from local school districts supplemented by often extensive local fund-raising activities—from across the country. The national circuit tournaments have the most prestige, and several—the annual tournaments at Berkeley, Emory, Harvard, Glenbrooks High School (outside Chicago), and the prestigious "Tournament of Champions" held in Lexington, Kentucky—sit atop them all. The national high school championship itself is conducted by the NSDA in June of each year and is open to only the top-performing teams from each state. For reasons to be explained, the style of debating and the background of the judges generally differs at state and national circuit tournaments.

BOX 2-1

Illustrating Competitive Policy Debate with
the 2018–2019 High School Debate Topic

The national high school policy debate topic for the academic year 2018–2019 could not have been timelier, given the sharp disputes about and lack of a national consensus on what course to take with respect to immigration: "Resolved: The United States federal government should substantially reduce its restrictions on legal immigration to the United States."

A variety of affirmative "cases" can be constructed around this resolution, ranging from a broad-based case in favor of loosening overall national immigration quotas to narrower cases focusing on specific types of immigrants, such as college or graduate students (especially those earning degrees in STEM subjects) or entrepreneurs (my personal favorite), or refugees. Presumably, the major "need" for these cases arises out of the quest for faster economic growth, which most immigrants would meet under any one of these "cases" or "criteria" by infusing new ideas and adding more talent and skills to our economy and society.

A "pure" negative case responding to any of these cases would not necessarily deny the need for more growth—a proposition that is difficult to defend—but could contend that the major challenge confronting our economy and society today is rising inequality, that (anticipating the affirmative plan) more immigrants would widen this disparity, and that increased inequality outweighs any benefits of added growth. Another negative attack could stress that additional immigration of any type threatens social cohesion, which is necessary for any society, let alone a democracy, to function.

Alternatively, the first negative could admit the need for more growth but offer a solution unrelated to loosened immigration for achieving it. For example, a counterplan could support even more or better targeted tax cuts, which, if tied to additional work (such as the Earned Income Tax Credit), could enhance both growth and equity. Or it might advocate a substantial boost in federally funded research and development as a way of boosting economic growth in the long run.

In response to either a conventional negative case or one that offered a counterplan, the second affirmative could claim—especially if the affirmative case is built around a narrower proposition, like letting in more STEM graduates from U.S. universities or foreign entrepreneurs—that loosened immigration is a lower-cost and less deficit-expanding way of boosting growth. As to the negative's claim that immigration of any sort would worsen inequality, the affirmative could respond that the expansion of business enabled by talented and highly driven immigrants would leave, at worst, income inequality where it is while boosting growth, thus making America better off.

Or, in response to a possible negative counterplan, the second affirmative speaker could offer a perm—a blend of the affirmative plan and counterplan, discussed in more detail in the chapter. For example, an affirmative plan to permit entry of more entrepreneurs could be combined with additional government spending on research and development. The second affirmative, presumably, would argue that this combination of proposals would produce faster growth than either plan alone.

The second negative must critique the affirmative's plan, or its perm. To counter an affirmative plan to grant more entrepreneurs' green cards (and a pathway to citizenship), for example, the second negative could argue that its threshold revenue or capital requirements for accepting immigrant entrepreneurs are too permissive, unrealistic, too easily circumvented, or administratively infeasible, or some combination of these claims. In rebuttal, the affirmative must be prepared to counter these objections or those to any other plan or case the affirmative puts forward.

Innovations and Changes in Policy Debate

Several strategic innovations have fundamentally changed policy debate over the last five decades. For what it's worth, I think the effects have been mixed. But before immersing into those details, keep in mind that this discussion is provided only as background for those who may be interested in competitive debate strategy. The kinds of arguments you are about to read about are not likely to be used in everyday classrooms, where I advocate that *basic* debate techniques already described should be used to teach most subjects more effectively.

The first strategic development since I debated is the much greater use by competitive debaters of "counterplans" by negative teams. A counterplan strategy concedes the need for change posited by the affirmative team but offers a different way to meet the need than is implied by the resolution. This is called the "counterplan." For example, suppose the resolution is that the "Federal government should adopt common sense gun control measures." A counterplan that doesn't invoke the solution implied by the resolution but one that would concede the need to do something about gun violence might take the form of proposing a major increase in funding for targeted mental health care for people at risk of using a gun to harm or kill. The debate then turns on which plan more effectively reduces gun violence.

Competitive debate is no different from other activities in life. People don't sit still after some change in the environment, including shifts in strategies and technologies. In the case of counterplans, second affirmatives have countered over the years with something called the "perm," short for "permutation," representing a recombination of the affirmative and negative plans in such a way that continues to uphold the desirability of adopting the resolution. Perms can take various forms but have this common element: adopt the counterplan *and* some or all of the affirmative's plan. The perm strategy can also be used to response to the "kritik," or "k" strategy, discussed next. This is a "we'll have our cake and eat it too" strategy and clearly can put the negative in a bind, having to argue that the addition of the affirmative's plan to its counterplan is of little or no incremental value and could or would entail disadvantages (substantive or political) that more than offset its value. Depending on the resolution and the nature of the affirmative's plan, the prospect that any counterplan can be permed makes the offering of a counterplan riskier than it was before perms were introduced (though counterplans still are used more frequently than they were decades ago).

A second strategy used by many teams is what lawyers call "slippery slope" arguments; others label them the "parade of horribles." If A happens, then B, C, and D, or the very worst-case scenario, will play out, which means that A must be unacceptable. For example, in a hypothetical debate over whether to withdraw from the World Trade Organization, one team may claim that withdrawal would increase tensions between the United States and China, already tense at this writing, to the point where a military conflict becomes inevitable. Furthermore, the team may assert—possibly with some justification given a pessimistic official assessment in 2018 of the U.S. military's relative capabilities vis-à-vis China—that because the United States would lose a conventional war to China, it would use nuclear weapons, which in turn would trigger a nuclear counterreaction and, hence, nuclear war. Competitive debaters through the years have conjured up nuclear war end endgames with much less seemingly relevant resolutions.

One fallacy of "parade of horribles" arguments, of course, is that while the individual steps leading to the worst-case outcomes may be logically linked, they are divorced from any context or probability. Debaters often tend to treat each of the links, and the ultimate outcomes, as certainties when, in fact, they are anything but. However, in debates judged by which teams win "on points"—or the totality of answered or unanswered arguments—probabilities can be easily ignored. Likewise, some economists through the years have been guilty of "parade of horribles" thinking when arguing against mounting government deficits, asserting that at one point they would trigger a "dollar strike" by foreign investors, namely a dumping of dollars and Treasury bonds on world markets, sending the values of both down and interest rates up, inducing a recession. While such a low probability event remains possible, the more likely outcome is one posited by my late long-time Brookings colleague and mentor Charles Schultze: a gradual crowding out of other worthy government expenditures by mounting interest costs (that at this writing now exceed the cost of the annual defense budget), which together contribute to somewhat higher or gradually increasing interest rates or modestly slower economic growth. I will not be recommending in later chapters that the parade of horribles thinking or argumentation be replicated through debate-centered instruction in a wide variety of subjects.

The third, and much more controversial, strategic innovation in competitive policy debate is the use of kritik argumentation (drawn from German philosophers' "kritiks"), which essentially ignores the debate resolution and puts competitive debate or the specific resolution itself on trial.[3] Advanced initially in the early 1990s, "k" arguments take many forms.[4]

One economic version is to advance the Marxist claim that capitalism is bad and, thus, any affirmative case that advances capitalism *ipso facto* also is bad. Another version has become especially popular, and successful at least in national circuit high school debates and on the college level: claims that competitive debate is racially, or at least socioeconomically, biased in that debaters from upper middle-class families in largely white suburban schools have more resources, both at home and at school, to pursue the activity. This is especially true with the rise of summer debate camps, which can cost upward of $5,000 for a two-week intensive debate experience before the actual debate season begins in the fall when school starts. Top debaters routinely attend these camps to hone their skills and to build a body of "evidence" they plan to use throughout the debate year. Although scholarships are available for minority students to attend these camps, such opportunities are limited. For all these reasons, students have ample real-world support for claims that black and Hispanic students start well behind their white suburban counterparts in the competitive debate "race" that commences once school begins.

Racially-based kritik argumentation is featured in the documentary on high school debate *Resolved*, aired on HBO in 2007, and in an excellent true account of black student debaters in Kansas City, Missouri, in the 2006 book *Cross-X*.[5] These popular treatments perhaps helped pave the way for the first time a race-based kritik strategy was used by the winning team at the college level, by debaters from Emporia State University in 2013. Five years later, one of the judges of that final round, Scott Harris, witnessed his team from Kansas University win the college national championship using a similar strategy. To my knowledge, no policy debate team at the high school level has won the national championship with a race-based or other kritik strategy, but some form of kritik is still widely used at the high school level.

I have mixed feelings about kritik arguments. On the one hand, there is no question that socioeconomic and racial differences among students and their family backgrounds contribute to an unlevel playing field in competitive debate, as is true throughout all aspects of life. This disparity in debate has been closed to some degree by open-source sharing of evidence developed at summer camps through the Open Evidence Project, a project launched by the National Debate Coaches Association in 2010 expressly for this purpose.[6] But socioeconomic differences affect performance in many other competitive activities at the high school and college levels—for example, in golf, tennis, and swimming—yet none of the basic rules for competitions in these sports have been challenged or changed as a result.

In effect, teams advancing kritik arguments are playing a different game than other teams that follow traditional debate conventions. It seems that teams showing up for basketball games against competitors who want to play football instead ought to be told "football is fine, but go play it elsewhere; just not here, and now." The debate equivalent would be to establish separate debate tournaments for teams wanting to duke it out over which kritik is better than the others. It also seems, however, that debate teams using kritik arguments that rely less on evidence than persuasion—even performance—almost certainly are more successful, on average, in many (but not all) debate competitions than they would be if they were limited to conventional debate strategies. This increase in success encourages more minority and perhaps even female participation in debate activities. If one believes, as I do, that debate develops educational and life skills, this results-oriented justification for kritik cannot be dismissed.

It is possible that kritik arguments will find a home in some classes, such as civics (government), history, or even English, when DCI becomes more widely used throughout the school curriculum. For example, it is impossible to ignore the role that issues of race stemming from America's sordid history of slavery have played a role in affecting racial relations and the economic and political opportunities open to black Americans to this day. But in general, race-based or other kritik arguments are not likely to play a central role in debate-centered education because the instructional method itself rules it out: students cannot challenge "the system" when asked to conduct research, present arguments, and respond to those arguments all based on evidence. That is precisely the point of the educational exercise, and criticism of it—unless tied to a specific topic where such critiques are relevant—has no role in the classroom.

Speed Debating: A Mixed Development at Best

In addition to the foregoing strategic innovations in policy debate, one major stylistic change in competitive debate over the past several decades—ever increasing speed—stems from a fourth strategic innovation, one that was beginning to surface in the late 1960s at the high school level and the early 1970s in college debate, but did not really become mainstream until later in the 1970s.

Fast talking or speed debate arose from a tactic called "spreading" that negative teams began using to attack affirmative cases. Competitive debates are judged in part—how much depends on the background of the judge—on how many arguments advanced are effectively "answered." Negative teams found that they could increase their odds of winning, especially with judges who scored debates more by "points" than overall persuasiveness of the debaters, simply by stating as many arguments or objections as they could, however well (or poorly) founded they might be, in the hope that affirmative teams simply would not be able to answer them all in the limited times allotted to each speaker. Spreading inevitably sped up debates, since the faster negative team members could talk, the more arguments they could advance, which, of course, required affirmatives to match or even exceed the speed of their opponents.

Today, it is not uncommon for competitive debaters to speak at 400 words per minute. In contrast, normal speech consists of about sixty words a minute. To see what a difference this makes, just type into any internet search engine "national high school debate championship" or "college national debate championship" and view just briefly the debates and the debaters who pop up. I defy any nondebater, or even most former debaters, to be able to discern much, if anything, of what the speakers are saying. To be fair, these debates are from "national circuit" tournaments at the high school level and advanced debaters (by definition) at the college level, most or all of whom have already mastered the "art" of speed debating. The pace of speaking at state high school tournaments can vary from round to round, although it is my impression that in the most competitive post-preliminary rounds, speed is the norm.

Good debaters learn to master debate at any speed and learn what pace to use by talking to judges beforehand to determine their debate background. If they are lay judges, then speed is to be avoided, but if the judges have debated before, especially in recent decades, they are more likely to want or even demand speed debating. As a broad generalization, speed debating is common at national circuit tournaments, where the rounds are judged by current or recent college debaters and debate coaches. As I discuss later in more detail, in college, teams at national circuit tournaments can rank order, within limits, those judges they reject before the competitive rounds begin and judges are formally assigned, at least during preliminary rounds. This removes some bias, but at the cost of making the contests even more of a game than they have long been. Most state-level tournaments are judged by lay individuals during preliminary rounds, who place more emphasis on style and persuasiveness than on points. Speed debating is, therefore, much less common at those tournaments, although it can surface during the championship rounds.

As with kritik argumentation, I am of two minds about speed debate. On the positive side, speaking and being able to react hyper-quickly is a real skill. But this is a skill, like highly competitive sports, that may be mastered by only a tiny percent of a school's student body. It is also a skill, as former debater Linda Listrom reminded me, that can be mastered only after you've mastered all the basics; you don't get to 400 words a minute (up from as high as 200 words when she and I were debating in college) without being able to articulate arguments at much lower speeds.

But a vast majority of students never will be competitive debaters, just as a smaller majority of students do not compete in interscholastic sports. Nonetheless, there is value in competing athletically in intramural sports, or just with your friends: using not only the physical activity and coordination and skills required for specific sports, but also learning teamwork. Honing the skills of debating at ordinary talking speed, however, is likely to have broader benefits, not only for students in their other classes but in stimulating interest in learning for its own sake, which has its own virtues. There may also be other collateral benefits of learning how to debate in a civil manner, at a normal speaking pace: such as reducing the propensity to engage in acts of violence, especially for young people who are frustrated in school and who live and go to school in violent neighborhoods where there is peer pressure to join gangs or to resort to physical intimidation rather than persuasion.

In short, speed debate is not the model for the debate-centered education whose widespread use I urge. Indeed, speed debating in competitive settings could make it more difficult to convince educators to adopt debate-centered education in other parts of the school curriculum. By going to YouTube and replaying the championship rounds of competitive policy debates, teachers, principals, and school members may be led into falsely equating speed debating with ordinary classroom debates constructed for their educational value and conducted at normal speaking speed.

Speed debating, with its emphasis on scoring points, also may fuel the criticism that debating does not encourage participants to seek "truth," as advanced by Jonathan Ellis and Francesca Hovagimian, two critics of conventional high school debating, in a *New York Times* op-ed in the fall of 2019.[7] While the authors acknowledge the educational and civic value of having to debate both sides of issues, they argue that the art of persuasion, which they claim debate develops, is not only inconsistent with the search for truth but corrodes our already divisive political discourse. I differ on several counts.

For one thing, as subsequent chapters show, the ability to persuade audiences is essential in many settings—even in science, where the search for truth is paramount—and is a skill that high school students can use in college and the workplace; indeed, throughout the rest of their lives. For another, the authors miss the mark when they fail to recognize that speed debating, which is how competitive policy debate and even other forms of debate have adapted, is not about persuasion but about simply scoring points. In addition, as I will argue at length, our political discourse is as distorted as it is in part because most of our electorate has no formal debate training, especially the ability to see the merits of and be able to convincingly persuade others of both sides of many issues.

If there is any drawback to competitive debating, it is not closing young minds to the search for truth but the very opposite: training young people to be too open-minded, a tendency some pick up precisely because they are compelled to debate both sides of a proposition, generally back-to-back in different "rounds" of competitive tournaments.[8] This effect is not as likely to materialize in less confrontational settings, like classrooms, where the pedagogical value of debate concepts—and the importance of supporting claims by evidence, reasoning, and effective rebuttal—have both presumptive and preliminarily proven educational value, as discussed in chapter 3.

Technology and Debate

Two other noteworthy innovations in policy debate relate to the use of technology. One important development is the introduction and now widespread use of laptop or tablet computers in debate competitions. Debaters use their portable devices to do real-time research during debates using standard search engines to check on claims made by the other side, to locate evidence the teams have already filed in relevant subject matter folders, and to structure their speeches. Indeed, it has become routine for debate participants to send outlines of their talks, complete with references to evidence backing their claims, by email to opposing teams and to judges.

The widespread use of computers undoubtedly improves the accuracy of debaters' claims and facilitates judging, especially by those trained in debating who score the debate by charting arguments and responses to them, or what debaters call judging "the flow." In the pre-computer era, debaters and judges mapped the flow of the debate on yellow legal pads. Word processing programs make this much easier. Since effective debating in this age requires the participants to be facile with word processing and internet search, debating promotes the learning of valuable computer-related skills that debaters carry with them into other classrooms and after they complete their formal schooling and enter the workforce.

The improvements in structure and evidence brought about by portable computers have come at a cost, however. They have removed some of the spontaneity and performance elements in debate. One day participants may ask what the point is of doing all this talking when we can simply exchange outlines and citations through email. I hope debate doesn't reach this point.

The second technological innovation represents a more fundamental challenge to policy debate, more than the other kinds to be discussed next. I refer here to the inevitable extension of artificial intelligence (AI) into debating—namely, having computers debate each other or, what has already occurred, computers debating humans. IBM, for example, has programmed computers to beat humans in chess and in the popular TV trivia game *Jeopardy*. It is moving in that direction with competitive debate, although computers have not yet been able to defeat one of the world's best human debaters.[9] But with further refinements, which are inevitable, IBM's Project Debater inevitably will master all human opponents.[10]

AI-driven debate may have the unintended benefit, however, of forcing policy debate to change—and slow down. Since computers ultimately will be better at "flow" than humans, enthusiasm for speed debate may dwindle, replaced by other forms of debate that put much more emphasis on persuasion, even emotion. Several of those forms already exist, as I discuss next. Others may develop in the future.

Other Forms of Debate: Slower, More Persuasive

Well before IBM's Project Debater was introduced, many in the high school and college debate communities were growing alarmed by the negative features of speed debate and began turning to alternative debate formats. One such alternative is "Public Forum" (PF) debate, which has several features that in combination put less emphasis on research and the speed reading of it and more on persuasive speaking skills.

In PF, the topics change every month rather than remaining the same throughout the school year, which broadens the range of issues debaters must research and discuss and, thus, inherently tips the scales away from research-intensive debating styles. The allotted times for the constructive and rebuttal speeches in PF are half those of policy debate, while the initial cross-examination periods allow both speakers to directly challenge each other (relabeled "cross-fire" rounds for this reason), and a closing crossfire round enables all four participants (two from each team) to engage in a free-for-all. While in recent years, some PF debaters have sped up their speaking speed, they generally do not talk as rapidly as policy debaters, because PF was developed primarily as one way to put more emphasis on persuasive speaking.

Another debate format that has evolved, in part in reaction to the speed of policy debate, is called the Lincoln-Douglas (LD) debate, named after the famous debates in the 1858 Illinois senate race between Senator Stephen Douglas and his challenger, Abraham Lincoln. Just as the original Lincoln-Douglas debates focused on the great moral question of its time—slavery—the LD debates today focus debaters on broad topics that entail value judgments along with logic and evidence. Sample LD topics have included whether the death penalty should be abolished, whether developing countries should prioritize environmental protection over resource extraction, and whether in a democratic society convicted felons should be able to vote (which voters in the state of Florida approved in 2018).

The format for LD debates differs even more substantially from policy debate than the PF debate form. LD debates pit only one person per team (rather than two) against each other. Accordingly, the debates feature only two constructive speeches (typically six to seven minutes long), two rebuttals, and cross examination of each speaker following each constructive presentation. LD topics change every two months, allowing a bit more time, and putting emphasis on research, for debaters to develop their cases and counterarguments than PF debate, but less than in competitive policy debate, where only a single resolution is contested throughout the school year.

Although kritik arguments have found their way into PF and LD debates, they tend to be less prominent than in policy debate, where a greater premium still is placed on evidence and speed rather than on persuasive speaking. For this reason, PF and LD competitive formats are more suitable analogies for the debates that now take place in classrooms where teachers use debate or argumentative techniques for instructional purposes, and for the kinds of instruction whose much wider use I will advocate in the next chapter in more detail and throughout the rest of this book.

British Parliamentary (BP) debate (often called World Schools debate at the high school level) has become increasingly popular, especially at the collegiate level where the format is used for an annual World Championship event. As its name suggests, BP debate is modeled after debating styles long used in the British Parliament, with the "Government" advancing a position and the "Opposition" countering it. Adapted to competitive debating, the version of BP debate used at the World Debate Championships, the most common form, has four individuals on each team who each make opening statements of up to seven minutes, with shorter rebuttals later. The debaters can interrupt each other, however, calling for "points of information" to clarify a statement of the current speaker.

Remarkably, participants in BP debate don't know their topics until fifteen minutes before the debate begins. This makes for a lot of tension and "hurry-up" preparations by both sides. It also requires preparation for a wide array of current policy issues, domestic and international, but much less emphasis on "evidence" and much more on logic and skills of persuasion than are evident in other debate formats, including LD and PF, where the topics are known in advance. The rapid speaking that has taken over PD won't be seen at BP debates, which, in my view, come closest to preparing students for real life—not just as elected officials but in a wide variety of occupations and workplace settings that call for spontaneous but thoughtful modes of argument and presentational skills.

At the high school level, congressional debate has developed as another format, but with Congress rather than Parliament as the model. High schools also host competitions in various speech and performance activities, including extemporaneous speaking (in which the participants deliver five-minute talks on topics given to them thirty minutes in advance), oratory, humorous interpretation, and informative speaking (speeches about topics chosen by the speaker and backed by evidence).

One Broad Critique of all Debate Formats

One critique of all debate formats, especially as debate has "sped up"—not only in PD but in other formats, too—relates to the fact that competitive debate encourages debaters to learn their judge's preferences in debating style (fast, very fast, or normal speaking rate, for example) by speaking to them in advance of the debate. In addition, college debate tournaments, and a few high school tournaments on the national circuit, allow debate teams (through their coaches) to rank order their preferences for specific judges, while ruling out others, before tournaments begin. The tournaments plug those rank orderings into a computer algorithm, which spits out judging assignments that are somewhat aligned with debate teams' styles. The assignments clearly are not random.

In effect, because competitive debaters can influence who judges them—though to a limited extent, because both sides can rule out certain judges, too—they can become adept in telling their audiences what the debaters think they want to hear. It sounds a lot like what's wrong with politics and many politicians today, doesn't it? Perhaps some of our better politicians who have had debate experience have used it in a cynical way to fuel their own personal ambition, not just following their voters preferences but manipulating them to feel so strongly about their positions that they are highly motivated to vote in the candidates' favor. Any such tendencies are likely to be most pronounced during primary campaigns when only the most motivated voters turn out. Might competitive debate experience for those politicians who have it in their backgrounds have made things worse? Why on earth would educators ever want to compel all high school students to develop such manipulation skills?

I'm not advocating the importation of these sometimes unpleasant sides of competitive debate into the classroom. When students debate in class, they can't pick their judge, who is the teacher. Some teachers allow other students to vote as well. Classroom debate enables the student to demonstrate a thorough understanding of the material relevant to the chosen topic—and more important, to develop and deepen that understanding—while developing skills of speaking and persuading audiences. Those benefits last a lifetime.

As for the charge that competitive debate may encourage some degree of manipulation, that may be true for some participants. But in my interviews with former debaters, the most common response to this charge is that competitive debate helped participants understand who they were talking to and to adapt their style and perhaps the substance of their argument to specific judges. This is a virtue, not a flaw. In real life, we can't always choose our audience, whether it be a boss or our peers. Acquiring the ability to detect what arguments will likely persuade listeners is a good skill to have.

Educational Benefits of Competitive Debate

As highlighted in the opening chapter, most if not all the skills taught and learned in competitive debating, under any format, should help debaters in all their educational activities and in all their coursework. These skills include the ability to research (with the aid of, but not exclusively confined to, the internet), to think logically; to back up arguments with evidence (not fake news!); to express one's thoughts in a persuasive, civil manner; and perhaps most important, the ability to argue and, thus, see the merits of both or multiple sides of most any issue or subject. These skills, especially in research, organization, and critical thinking, are important not only in a wide range of formal classes but throughout life. While they help structure an individual's belief systems—a set of principles or stories of how we each make sense of the world—debate skills also help one keep an open mind, be receptive to new ideas, and understand the tradeoffs that are necessary to allow democratic institutions and systems to function.

Because it is mentally challenging, debate also forces participants to listen to what the other side is saying, while formulating responses that an independent audience—whether a teacher, a potential employer, a supervisor, or a voter—is likely to find most persuasive. Good debaters must be prepared for challenges to their positions and be prepared to meet them. Good lawyers do this all the time, conducting mock arguments or cross-examinations that prepare them for all possible counterarguments to their own. This requires attorneys to learn the facts and the law of their case thoroughly before explaining it to a judge or a jury. Students prepare to defend their undergraduate or Ph.D. theses before individual professors or a panel of them in much the same way. So do CEOs preparing for board meetings, or lower level executives preparing to report to their bosses. The list goes on.

There is an academic literature in debate and communications journals, generally authored by debate and speech teachers and coaches who are former debaters themselves, purporting to demonstrate that participation in competitive debate enhances all these skills and, thus, helps participants in their formal schooling and throughout their lives. Advocates of the lifetime benefits of debate often point to the success of luminaries today—such as those listed in the appendix to chapter 1—who were once competitive debaters.

There is a major shortcoming to virtually all this literature, however. The typical studies that compare the educational performance of competitive debaters versus other students, or that compare the performance of debaters before and after their participation in the activity, make no attempt to control for the possibility, if not the likelihood, that many debaters are attracted to the activity because they already are facile speakers, highly intelligent, or both. As previewed in the opening chapter, social scientists call this selection bias, and if it is not somehow controlled for, studies cannot really determine whether debaters who do well in school or later in life did so because they had debated or whether they were already predisposed to do well in both debate and in the rest of their lives. In other words, without the proper controls, there is no way to identify the true value added by debate (apart from any fun, as well as the anxieties, the participants probably had in engaging in the activity).

Chapter 1 provides several personal stories or anecdotes, making it clear that at least in these instances, self-selection was not responsible for the transformational impact of competitive debate. As the old joke goes, the plural of anecdotes is "data." The dozens of interviews conducted in the research for this book provide additional data points rebutting the self-selection explanation for the value of competitive debate. In any event, even if some self-selection was at work, competitive debate refined and honed the speaking and thinking skills of participants who already may have been predisposed to debate competitively.

Policymakers and educators are not likely to take bold action because of dozens of such stories, nor should they. Before a major policy intervention is tried or scaled, there should be harder statistical evidence that it is likely to work—although unfortunately, policymakers have not always adhered to that principle.[11] I will hold myself to a higher standard in arguing for expanding the pedagogical reform that is the subject of this book: combining the best available statistical evidence with anecdotal evidence and logic.

It is now widely recognized by scientists, in both the "hard" and "soft" sciences, that one of the best ways to control for self-selection is to design and conduct an experiment, randomly assign people to participate in it, and then compare outcomes along some suitable metrics of those who receive the "treatment" versus those that don't. Such randomized controlled trials (RCTs) are the standard way the Food and Drug Administration requires drug manufacturers to test the safety and efficacy of new medications before they can be sold. Economists and other social scientists are increasingly using RCTs to test the efficacy of various policy or business practice innovations, including different educational policies (charter schools) or pedagogical techniques or supplements (such as text reminders to students and parents).[12] As noted in the preface, the use of RCTs in social sciences, especially in economics, was validated by the award of the 2019 Nobel prize to three economists who pioneered the use of the technique in studying various ways to reduce poverty in developing countries.

So far, however, no school district has experimented with an RCT to test for educational and other possible benefits of participation in competitive debate, such as the effects on post-school earnings or mental health or the propensity toward violence rather than conversation to resolve disputes, most likely for several reasons. For one thing, to my knowledge no school district has been presented with the idea. Also, even if the idea were proposed, cost as well as ethical and political objections surely would be raised by students and their parents (Why should I be denied the ability to participate in debate simply by chance?) and even by debate coaches fearful of losing their jobs or not wanting to switch schools solely for the purpose of carrying out the experiment. These reasons do not mean, however, that RCTs can't or won't be used in the future to test the efficacy of curriculum reforms motivated by debate, as is discussed in the next chapter.

Fortunately, there is an alternative way to control for self-selection, using data from all students who have participated in debate. Statisticians are used to having bodies of data representing outcomes and then being asked how they can be "explained." Rarely can they say, empirically or even theoretically, that only one force, trend, or event is responsible. Rather, the world is complicated and so are outcomes like health and educational and economic performance, as measured by any number of variables. Statisticians take account of such multiple driving forces through multiple regression analysis, a technique for fitting an equation to a body of data, using multiple explanatory variables. One or more of those variables can serve as a proxy variable to measure the likelihood of self-selection.

In the competitive debate context, Professor Briana Mezuk, now an epidemiologist at the University of Michigan (then at Virginia Commonwealth University) and three coauthors did this in a study of high school students who debated competitively from 1997 through 2006 in the Chicago Debate League—which is part of the National Association of Urban Debate Leagues previewed in the first chapter.[13] The researchers compared the educational performance of debaters and nondebaters in the Chicago Public School district at the same schools that participated in the Chicago Urban Debate League. They controlled for self-selection by calculating a debate propensity score based on eighth-grade standardized test scores. That measure is not perfect because it takes no account of the students' speaking abilities, but test scores are rough measures of the combination of intelligence and prior educational achievement and learning, which are important for success in competitive debate.

Mezuk and her colleagues found that even *after accounting for the influence of self-selection,* the debaters were "more likely to graduate from high school, performed better on the ACT, and showed greater gains in cumulative GPA relative to similar comparison students." Former debaters are not at all surprised at this result given the multiple skills that competitive debaters must acquire and, ideally, master. But the researchers do not attribute their positive results solely to cognitive improvements enabled by participation. The researchers also attribute debate's positive impacts to the fact that the activity "*promote(s) engagement* with scholastic materials in a manner that translates into academic performance" (emphasis added).[14] The motivational aspect of debate is an important element of the activity, as argued in the next chapter, that can and should benefit many more students who are exposed to debate in a noncompetitive, schoolroom environment as well.

Mezuk has continued her study of debaters with different researchers and found reinforcing positive conclusions from participation in competitive debate. Her follow-up analyses have also found that high-school debaters have higher social, civic, and school engagement[15] and are more likely to matriculate to college than nondebaters.[16]

It is not necessary to wait for students to be in high school for them to reap the benefits of competitive debate. As part of his Ph.D. thesis at Johns Hopkins, Daniel Shackelford analyzed school performance data of competitive debaters at the elementary (beginning in 4th grade) and middle school levels in Baltimore from 2004 into 2014. He controlled for self-selection not only through standardized test scores but also school attendance rates, the latter to capture engagement with learning. Shackelford's findings are similar to those reported in the studies by the various Mezuk-led research teams examining high school debaters.[17]

Specifically, Shackelford concludes that debaters had better test scores in reading and math and better grades than nondebaters. Debaters also were more likely to attend high schools having entrance requirements, which Shackelford shows have substantially higher graduation rates than conventional Baltimore schools. These findings are especially noteworthy for urban school districts where large fractions of middle schoolers never make it to high school or drop out before they graduate the 12th grade. Shackelford's results document that participation in competitive debate even well before high school can truly change the life trajectories of minority students from disadvantaged backgrounds who can be subjected to strong peer pressure to do the wrong things, by keeping them on a path toward high school graduation and academic excellence.

If competitive debate is likely to enhance educational performance for its participants, a natural question arises: Can forms of debate that emphasize persuasive and logical thinking be used to benefit all students, not just the relative handful who compete? Readers should not be surprised at my affirmative answer. The next three chapters demonstrate why the benefits to individual students, the economy, and our democracy are potentially substantial.

THREE

Beyond Competition

Debate-Centered Instruction for All

Until several decades ago, Americans could be and were reasonably proud of their K–12 system of education. The United States was among the first countries to institutionalize education through high school. In the first few decades after World War II, literacy rates, high school graduation, and college attendance and graduation rates in this country were among the highest in the world. Overall, the American educational system turned out record numbers of Nobel-prize winners (many winners were immigrants), an enviable record of scientific achievement and business success.

But sometime in the 1970s, if not earlier, and certainly by the early 1980s, other nations' school systems caught up to and even surpassed the United States on various performance measures. By 1983, a distinguished presidential commission appointed by President Reagan and headed by David Gardner, Secretary of Education during the Johnson administration, sounded an alarm about the state of American K–12 education that was evident simply from the title of its report: *A Nation at Risk.*[1]

The report pointed to rapidly declining standardized test scores of students, the fact that nearly 40 percent of seventeen-year-olds could not successfully "draw inferences from written material," and "only one-fifth can write a persuasive essay; and only one-third can solve a mathematics problem requiring several steps." These poor results contributed to the poor international ranking of U.S. high schoolers at the time, as well. The commission advanced several recommendations, including a longer school day and year; higher, performance-based salaries for teachers; and tougher college admissions standards to counteract grade inflation.

A Nation at Risk sparked a multi-decade wave of educational reform efforts, including the launching of "charter" public schools that are free of many of the constraints of conventional public schools; a variety of pedagogical changes in schools; the enactment by Congress of the No Child Left (NCLB) Behind Act of 2001 and the Every Student Succeeds Act of 2015, which largely overturned the NCLB; the development of the "Common Core" national standards and subsequent backing away from those standards in certain states; and a lot of academic studies, which the Department of Education ultimately began to catalog and make public on its "What Works" website.[2] Many of these reform efforts and their assessments have been funded by various foundations.

One would expect that the multiple reforms would have improved U.S. education. However, although there are pockets of improvements here and there, the overall assessment is far from encouraging.

For example, the most widely watched national standardized test scores, those from the National Assessment of Educational Progress (NAEP), show that while reading and math scores of nine- and thirteen-year-olds were 8 to 25 points (on a 350-point scale) higher in 2012 than in 1971, the first year the NAEP tests were administered, for students age seventeen, *no improvement* over the thirty-year period was evident.[3] An NAEP report issued in 2019 showed 8th graders backsliding in both reading and math, with mixed results for 4th graders, who scored a bit higher in reading and a bit lower in math.[4]

The results from internationally standardized tests are equally disappointing. The two dominant international tests are the Program for International Student Assessment (PISA) and the Trends in International Mathematics and Science Study (TIMSS). PISA, first administered in 2000, tests samples of fifteen-year-old students in reading, math, and science every three years. TIMSS has been administered to 4th and 8th graders since 1995 and tests them in math and science. Both tests are designed to test for achievement, not aptitude, like the SAT or ACT college entrance exams for high school students in the United States.[5]

The latest year as of this writing for which results from both tests are available is 2015, and both tell the same story as the U.S.-based NAEP tests tell: while the TIMSS test scores for younger students have improved over the past two decades, the scores for the older students have been flat. The United States ranks, at best, in the middle of the pack of other rich countries.

In short, for decades since *A Nation at Risk* was released, the U.S. K–12 system overall has modestly improved for younger students but is somehow failing to translate those improvements to older students or to those in high school—the student population that is the focus of much of this book. Americans seem to know this already and, by a large majority, fear things will only get worse. A Pew Research survey in March 2019 reported "that 77% of Americans worry about the ability of public schools to provide a quality education to tomorrow's students, and more expect the quality of these schools to get worse, not better, by 2050."[6]

To be fair, test scores are not everything. Critics say that the focus on test scores, which the NCLB legislation elevated in importance, has distorted education, compelling teachers to teach to the test, driving out creativity as well as time spent on nonmath and English subjects, including history, arts, language, and music. My impression from reading the education literature is that while much of this appears to be true, judging by the actual test score results, teaching to the test hasn't worked very well either.

The concern with the general state of education in America, however, conceals the progress and special challenges of various subgroups. This chapter will focus on three distinct student populations with very different characteristics but whose educational performance and life prospects are all capable of being improved through the same pedagogical reform outlined in this chapter: DCI.

One group is minority students, who typically attend inner city urban schools but also are found in schools in rural parts of the country, especially the South, whose performance has long lagged that of students in higher income, less diverse suburban areas. Although by some measures, the achievement gap between white and black American students in particular has narrowed somewhat since the Supreme Court's landmark decision over fifty years ago in *Brown v. Board of Education,* stubborn and unacceptable differentials persist. A landmark 2018 study by ProPublica documents the racial disparities that continue in the South and in large school districts. In Los Angeles and Chicago, black students, on average, are three school grades behind their white counterparts.[7]

A very different sort of challenge confronts students at the opposite end of the socioeconomic spectrum—largely white students attending high-performance but also high anxiety-producing suburban schools. On the surface, these students do well on tests, earn high (though often inflated) grades, and go on to college, dominating attendance at prestigious private universities. But a look below the surface, and on college campuses themselves, reveals problems that are different from those plaguing their high school educations.

In their important book *The Coddling of the American Mind,*[8] Greg Lukianoff and Jonathan Haidt show how too many students from this privileged demographic have been too sheltered, by their parents and society at large, in their formative years—but especially in their middle and high school years—from activities in and out of school that threaten their physical and emotional safety. As a result, middle and upper-middle class Americans are raising a generation of students—the "I-generation"—who are not well equipped to deal with the multiple intellectual and emotional challenges they inevitably must face when they leave the womb of their parents' comfortable homes to attend college. It is not surprising, therefore, when they get there that too many of them are afraid and unwilling to tolerate views that pose even the slightest risks to their feelings—"micro-aggressions"—let alone be willing to accept speakers or even teachers who challenge their world views. At the same time, because they have learned by high school to rely on third parties rather than to work things out among themselves, it is also not surprising that too many make demands on college administrators who because they, too, have become risk averse, are all too willing to accommodate them. In short, our society and our educational institutions are doing a suboptimal job at best of readying the next generation for the rough-and-tumble of the workforce, let alone the growing incivilities of our politics.

The third group on which this chapter will focus is girls, who have consistently outperformed boys in school to the point where many observers now openly worry about boys' difficulties in school. I'm not as worried about that because the pedagogical reform discussed later in this chapter and throughout the rest of this book should help motivate boys to do better and to be more engaged in school. But I don't want that to happen at the expense of girls, who despite their ascendance in school performance, still face an important challenge: speaking up.

Sheryl Sandberg, chief financial officer of Facebook, popularized the problem that girls—and grown women—must overcome in life, and that is to become more self-assertive, or to "lean in."[9] From an early age, girls are more reluctant than boys to speak up in class. Those who do, in school and eventually in the workplace, are more likely to be viewed by other girls and boys (men) as self-centered or more nakedly ambitious than males. This disparity helps explain why even though girls have overtaken boys in educational achievement and have made progress toward achieving greater equality—in the voting booth, at work, and in their incomes—women still are underrepresented in corporate boardrooms and in political office (although that latter disparity has closed significantly since 2016 and with the rise of the "Me Too" movement, with record numbers of women running for and winning elected positions at all levels of government).

Bookshelves and magazine racks are full of suggestions advanced by experts from many fields, including corporate and political leaders, on how best to tackle the educational challenges confronting each of these groups, as well as to improve American K–12 education in general. Among the more prominent suggestions are to lift teacher pay (generally or selectively, such as higher pay for teaching in schools in socioeconomically disadvantaged areas) and fostering the growth of "good" public charter schools while more aggressively weeding out poorly performing charters. I do not see a need to weigh the pros and cons of these and other reform ideas, because the main suggestion offered here—implement DCI more widely throughout *all* schools—remains relevant whatever one's views may be about other reforms.

Nonetheless, there is one reform—the adoption and implementation of Common Core education standards—that is relevant to my recommendation. Although the Common Core standards have come under attack from multiple directions, it is important to remember how they came about. In the late 1990s, leaders from the business and education communities were widely dissatisfied with our K–12 education system (as many still are), as were governors from both political parties. There was a consensus then, as I believe there should be today, that one element in improving education is to ensure that students throughout the country are learning essentially the same material, so that all of them are potentially ready to participate in a national workforce.

But rather than impose such standards from the top down by the federal government—which has always had a back seat to local and state governments in educating our children and likely always will— these Common Core standards were developed from the ground up by the National Governors Association and the Council of Chief State School Officers, with input from a broad spectrum of educational organizations, including teachers' unions, and over 10,000 individuals who submitted comments to a draft version of the standards. The intent was to have the states implement the standards once they were finished, as they were in 2010. Ultimately, over forty states did so.[10]

Ironically, the Common Core had its political and intellectual roots in attempting to avoid what became one of the criticisms of the No Child Left Behind Act—that it delegated to the states both the standards and the materials students were to be taught and the principal means by which this was to be enforced, which meant there would be no way to objectively assess how students were performing across the country. The originators of Common Core wanted at least to have a national system of standards in place so that students in different states would not be taught and tested on different bodies of knowledge.

The ink was hardly dry on Common Core, however, before a backlash began. The main critique—that the standards encroached on state control of education—was advanced even before the Obama administration endorsed the standards and made compliance with them a component of its "Race to the Top" education grants to the states promising the most innovative ways to improve education. The fact that the standards were developed under the auspices of state governors and adopted by almost all states in the country did not stop some states later from backing away from their commitments to implement the standards, as the debate over the standards themselves turned highly political. Even so, as of 2017, thirty-five states still adhered to the original standards, but eleven states have modified them in some fashion.[11]

This history is relevant to the main education reform discussed and endorsed in this chapter and in the book. One central but little-noticed feature of the standards was their emphasis on students engaging in critical thinking and reasoning, a feature that figured prominently in the revision of the SAT college entrance exam, in the added essay and in its traditional verbal portion.[12] The commonality between the Common Core and the new SAT is not an accident: the same individual, David Coleman, was heavily involved in both efforts. Coleman had personal experience in the world of competitive debate as an early board member of the New York Urban Debate League and as an advisory board member of the National Association for Urban Debate Leagues.

But there was nothing in the Common Core (nor the revised SAT) that counseled teachers *how* to teach the material that made up the standards, other than several broad directions to train students to make and refute arguments and demonstrate the capacity to evaluate competing claims and the evidence that supports them, in their reading of texts, in their writing assignments, and in listening to speakers. Citing scholar Neil Postman, one of the research appendices to the Standards notes that "argument is the soul of an education."[13]

Nor do the Common Core standards provide any guidance on the important related issue of how to engage students in wanting to learn, a skill and habit that affects the willingness to engage in lifelong learning, which in chapter 5 I argue is critical to workforce success and, hence, personal happiness in the twenty-first century. Student engagement, in and beyond formal schooling, in learning is also central to addressing the challenges posed by each of the three distinct student groups identified at the outset of this chapter.

Whatever your views may be about the content of the Common Core standards or whether and to what extent your state should implement them, the importance of the argumentation skills they emphasize cannot be overstated. Knowing how to construct arguments to defend your positions and to respond to critiques is helpful not only in school but throughout life, in the workplace and at home.

But why should these skills be limited to written expressions; or in the case of oral presentations, why should students be able to evaluate arguments and the evidence that backs them only as they listen? Shouldn't all students be able to make and counter arguments as they *speak,* a skill that right now in virtually all schools only competitive debaters learn to hone? If competitive debate is successful in motivating students to learn, to think critically as they are acquiring knowledge, and thus to understand more of what they are taught—as the evidence (and logic) reviewed in the last chapter suggest it has—why should these benefits be limited to just the relative handful of students in each school that has a debate program? The answer, of course, is that there is no good reason for any of these limits. In that simple insight lies a potential revolution in the way all students should be taught.

An Introduction to Debate-Centered Instruction

The twenty-first century is already presenting current workers with enormous challenges, as continuing shifts in consumer demand and preferences, advances in technology, and, despite some recent policy roadblocks, increasing globalization are constantly changing what workers need to know and learn to attain or maintain the standard of living to which they aspire. Much thought has been given to how future generations of workers—starting with students in school now—must be educated to survive and, ideally, thrive in this challenging environment. The National Education Association, the nation's largest union representing public school teachers and support personnel, has prepared a thoughtful report distilling what students need to know into what it calls the "4Cs"—critical thinking, communication, collaboration, and creativity. The report also provides illustrative ways teachers can impart these skills in the classroom, from K–12.[14] It is interesting, however, that nowhere does the report mention debate or the obvious connection that three debate skills—critical thinking, communication, and collaboration—overlap with the 4Cs. Arguably, good debaters are also creative, so debate satisfies all four of the Cs.

Yet as readers certainly know by this point, I do not believe that school should limit the development of debate skills just to competitive debaters. Rather, in high school and, ideally, well before, all students should benefit in most of their subjects (perhaps even math) from DCI.

This is not just my idea, nor is it new. Protagoras of Abdera, who earned his living teaching young Greeks how to argue in court settings over 2,400 years ago, is probably the "father of debate" as a method of instruction.[15] Plato and Socrates taught their students, not just in legal settings, "rhetoric" and argumentation. Much later, great thinkers

John Locke, Jean-Jacques Rousseau, and John Stuart Mill supported or proposed or used debate techniques to instruct their students in a wide variety of subjects.

Teaching young people, one-on-one or in small groups, how to learn through debating is easy compared to doing it on a mass scale in modern classrooms of thirty or more students. But that is precisely what several academic scholars began suggesting as early as the late 1980s.[16] In 2000, debate and communications professor Joe Bellon reinvigorated this suggestion, calling for debate in its oral form "across the curriculum"—essentially in all liberal arts subjects, including science—just as writing and even "communication" and "speech" had been implemented across subjects in many schools before.[17]

Debate is much more than just learning how to speak, however. Debate requires both effective listening and the ability to present one's views on virtually any topic, backed by evidence and logic, and then to defend those views orally when attacked, in real time, in a civil way. In structured debate, there is no name calling or shouting or interrupting, the mode of debate one sees all too often on cable television. Nor are there "flop accounts" on Instagram, which teens have used to debate serious issues but without rules; not surprisingly, those debates have since mirrored the incivility we see in real life and, unfortunately, far too often on the internet.[18]

Perhaps the most important benefit of debate is that it requires learning how to argue to both, or potentially multiple, sides of almost any issue, a skill that fosters critical thinking, empathy, and understanding for other positions, and an understanding of complexity— that most issues and questions in life are not "black" or "white" (in the nonracial sense of these terms), but involve shades of gray.[19] Understanding and appreciating this complexity is important to sharpening critical thinking while in school, but having this skill and experience is essential when students grow up to be voting and, ideally, thinking citizens (chapter 4), to be effective employees in all kinds of jobs, and even as entrepreneurs (chapter 5).

The early academic advocates of debate across the curriculum—

what I call here DCI—outlined the case for it primarily in high school, and not earlier, or later. With a few exceptions, however, they didn't wrestle with the logistics of how to implement the idea beyond the suggestion that class members, divided into teams, would debate a specific topic relevant to the course at the end of the semester—the oral equivalent of an end-of-course written paper. One very recent exception is provided in a textbook coauthored by Diana Carlin, an expert on presidential debates who has used debate as an instructional device in nearly all her classes as a high school teacher and at the college level.[20]

But outside of Carlin's use of debate in the classroom, it took some time for education reformer-innovators to experiment with ways of implementing debate as a method of instruction at middle and high school levels *throughout* an entire semester (or year-length) class. Two pioneers who are leading this effort today are Les Lynn, in Chicago, and Mike Wasserman, who heads the Boston Debate League. Both are former competitive debaters.

The pioneers of DCI (Lynn and the BDL use other labels for it) were influenced by academic scholars who had written about the importance of argumentation in learning,[21] but nonetheless each had to flesh out the mechanics of the idea from scratch, experimenting as they went along, sensing what seemed to work with teachers and their students and what didn't. Lynn and Wasserman knew of each other but hadn't met when I discovered them during my research for this book. The techniques they each developed have turned out to be quite similar. I envision those who adopt DCI in their schools continuing to experiment with and refine the techniques that Lynn and the BDL have developed.

DCI also should be viewed as one form of continuous PBL, championed by author and education reformer Ted Dintersmith and encouraged by PBLworks, led by its executive director Bob Lens.[22] Dintersmith makes a powerful case in his book that the current "factory based" model for K–12 education, which puts a premium on rote memory and test-taking skills—with some notable exceptions profiled in his book—

not only has taken the fun out of learning but ill equips students of today for the workplace challenges of tomorrow.

In a society where machines and software will be doing more and more "work," humans add value by working with artificial intelligence (AI) rather than being worried about being replaced by it. Meeting that challenge will require all workers to be creative, to think critically, and to communicate in ways that Alexa or Google Home cannot and never will be able to do. When students learn by applying their creativity to specific projects, using the tools of the internet and AI, they not only will appreciate learning but be better able to adapt to the needs of a constantly changing workplace, as discussed in the next chapter. Perhaps most important of all, students engaged in projects in innovative settings have fun and so are engaged in learning for the sake of learning that they want to come to school and do not view it as a chore or some rite of passage that adults command them to go through before the students themselves become adults. DCI, when implemented the right way, can do all that and more.

DCI in the Classroom

To gain an understanding of what DCI is and is not, it is useful to begin by reviewing how DCI has been implemented over an extended period by Lynn and the BDL.

A former high school and college debater, Les Lynn was a highly awarded high school teacher before founding the Chicago Debate League and then serving as the founding executive director of the National Association of Urban Debate Leagues. In 2009, he began working with the Chicago school system to train its teachers, where he first developed materials for applying what he later called "argument centered education" (ACE)—equivalent to the DCI concept I recommend here—throughout the middle and high school educational curriculum. In 2013, Lynn launched a consultancy to concentrate on "debatifying" the curriculum and training teachers specifically in ACE. To date, he has worked with over 3,000 teachers, of whom several hundred have been trained intensively in ACE techniques. As of 2019, Lynn was using ACE to work with schools throughout the Chicago Public School system to debatify their curricula and to train more than 300 teachers from eleven middle and high schools in Chicago and its suburbs, Northwest Indiana, and New York City in ACE-based instructional techniques.

Mike Wasserman and his colleagues at the Boston Debate League are also DCI pioneers. Currently the executive director of the BDL, Wasserman is also a former high school debater and high school debate coach. He initially joined the BDL as a board member and later was promoted to his current position, in which he has helped disseminate the BDL's version of DCI, which the BDL now calls "Debate in the Classroom" (changed from "evidence-based argumentation"). The BDL has helped teachers introduce debate concepts in fourteen Boston area schools as a school-level initiative, while training teachers in the technique across Massachusetts and Rhode Island. At last count, the league was providing multiyear, intensive instructional coaching and ongoing support to 600 teachers, reaching 6,000 students annually. The BDL team members believe Debate in the Classroom has helped turn around the performance of several schools they work with, helping them achieve the largest and fastest gains in school performance of any schools in the Boston Public School district.

Lynn's and the BDL's are not the only efforts to apply debate learning across the curriculum. The Urban Debate Leagues of Dallas and Houston also have similar mandates to support the teaching of debate in multiple classroom settings.

So how does DCI (or the other names it has been given) work? At a very general level, Lynn provides some specific answers in posts on his blog *The Debatifier*.[23] He recommends that teachers start with an open, debatable question on an issue central to a unit they are teaching, asking students to "read and study content in order to stake out a position on the issue and build evidence-based arguments that develop and support that position."[24] His mantra: state a claim, provide evidence to back it up, and then explain the reasoning supporting your claims. The BDL uses the same three-phase mantra in the work it does with its schools in Boston. The "claim-evidence-reasoning" linkage, coupled with the ability to respond to critiques, can also be found in the academic literature on how to apply debate techniques in the classroom.

Choosing the topics to be debated is probably the most important part of implementing DCI, and the one that offers the most room for experimentation and innovation by individual teachers. Broadly speaking, there are two basic approaches to picking topics:

- Consult outside sources that provide topics centered around "units"—typically three- to four-week sessions on a topic, such as a particular novel in English or a period of history in a civics or history class.

- Develop arguments around units that teachers are already teaching.

Both Lynn and the BDL strongly favor and have used the latter approach because it requires only a modification of the method of instruction already used by teachers but does not require them to master and teach new content that may not be part of the curriculum schools or their school boards have already chosen.

"Argumentalizing" (another Lynn coinage) preexisting units requires effort, although as with mastering any new material, most of the work is concentrated during the first year a teacher uses DCI. Effective delivery of DCI also greatly benefits from having an outside "argument" or debate-centered education "coach," at least for some initial period, like Lynn or Wasserman (or his staff members), to train teachers how to come up with topics and how to implement them.

Some topic examples for debates in high school are provided in the accompanying box, drawn from a two-week planning period during late April 2019 overseen by Lynn at Proviso West High School just outside of Chicago. It also can be useful to ask the students in the class what topics they would prefer to debate within a given unit, although because of students' unfamiliarity with the material until it is actually delivered, it probably would be best to solicit student input by giving them a range of teacher-selected topics once teachers and students have enough confidence in debate techniques to make good topic choices.

Some topics also may be perennials, capable of being used yearly, especially in English and history courses. These topics can be included in a library of sources that teachers can consult once DCI has become firmly embedded in a school. Lynn has been steadily building such a library for the Chicago schools he works with, and so has the BDL in partnership with its growing community of teacher leaders for the Boston area schools advised by the BDL.

Whatever the topics chosen, the main purposes of DCI, in whatever form it is used, should be to make students comfortable with making and expressing arguments and to do this in a way that separates the arguments from the identity of the person making them. Adam Grant of the University of Pennsylvania's Wharton School summarized, perhaps unintentionally, what DCI is all about when he wrote: "Instead of trying to prevent arguments, we should be modeling courteous conflict and teaching kids how to have healthy disagreements." He adds the following rules:

- Frame [the question] as a debate, rather than a conflict.

- Argue as if you're right but listen as if you're wrong.

- Make the most respectful interpretation of the other person's perspective.

- Acknowledge where you agree with your critics and what you've learned from them.[25]

Virtually any important topic in most courses can be converted into a debate, requiring participants to read the relevant works and also to do ancillary research, and then to make persuasive arguments on both sides of the question, as well as counter opposition in a civil manner.

BOX 3-1

Illustrative Classroom Debate Topics

Is the value of a four-year college degree
worth the cost? (Civics, English)

In *A Thousand Splendid Suns* by Khaled Hosseini, are
the female protagonists feminist heroes? (English)

What is the best way to reform America's asylum
system for immigration? (Civics, history)

Did the United States have to enter World War I? (History)

Do the benefits of DNA testing outweigh the risks? (Biology)

How best can all nations—rich and poor—be persuaded to
adopt less carbon-intensive technologies as a way of addressing
climate change? (Social studies, physics, international relations)

The opioid crisis is better handled through treatment programs
than through the criminal justice system. (History, civics)

What is the best way to solve any math problem
(ideally a word-based problem)? (Math)

Source: Les Lynn and Proviso West High School teachers participating in its ACE program and author.

As the box illustrates, the topics need not and should not be limited to the humanities. Debates exist because there is no settled answer about a specified topic, and that includes some topics in science. As the BDL has shown, and as Harvard physics professor Eric Mazur urges, students in science classrooms can be found debating a variety of scientific topics, such as the most significant cause leading to the extinction of the dinosaurs, increased volcanic activity, or the changing climate.

Certain BDL-mentored teachers also use the "claim-evidence-reasoning" paradigm drawn from debate to teach math, especially word problems, which require reasoning. In these situations, students are asked to identify the key assumptions behind the problem before outlining and then use a mathematical formula or math reasoning to solve the problem. Boston teachers told me that they find it helpful to use student answers that are mistakes (without identifying the student, of course) by showing them to the class and having the students debate where the student making the mistake went wrong. Another way to debatify math is to ask students the various ways a problem can be solved since, often, there are two or more ways to come up with the solution to a math problem or puzzle.

A variety of other issues arise and must be resolved or, perhaps better, subjected to continuous experimentation when schools are introducing DCI into their classrooms. For example, should the students be limited to using only the "evidence" supplied by the teacher (assisted by the school's argument or debate-centered education coach), or should the students be allowed or encouraged to research and use outside sources? The easy answer is to start with teacher-provided materials and only later—once students are familiar with debate techniques—consider whether to permit outside sources. Once students are encouraged to use third-party sources, however, they must be instructed in what sources are acceptable and which are not, a topic addressed more fully in chapter 6. The use of third-party sources also depends on the availability of computers in a school or at home. Clearly, schools with more resources, and with student populations from higher income families, will be in a better position to encourage independent research, though even "rich schools" will have students from lower income backgrounds without access to the internet at home who would be put at a disadvantage if third-party sources are allowed.

Another central issue is how students should best acquire debate skills. My initial thought when beginning to write this book was that students would gain the skills in a basic speech course, which teaches rhetoric, logic, and research skills—the same kind of course competitive debaters take, but without the competition—as early as the 9th or 10th grads—before taking other classes where debate techniques are used to teach the material. But Lynn and the BDL demonstrated to me during my visits to Chicago and Boston, and through further discussions, that this level of intense preparation is unnecessary.

The BDL, for example, has worked with the Boston school district to devote a portion of the district's professional development budget to funding a one-week (40-hour) accredited graduate course during the summer that the BDL offers to participating teachers. Following this course, the BDL embeds instructional coaches in each partner school, as Lynn himself does in Chicago. The instructional coach provides consulting and technical support for teachers using debate techniques in their classrooms.

It may not be economically feasible for school districts to fund or operate summer teaching training, which means that teachers and students must learn DCI skills as they go, in small doses, in the various classes in which argument-based learning is used. This is how Proviso West has introduced argument-centered education, with Lynn's assistance; over time, as teachers gain experience with the technique, less experimentation may be required.

It also may be useful, if not necessary, to begin with debate-styled seminars before asking students to formally debate. These seminars can be modeled after the Harkness table seminars used for several decades in some of the nation's leading elite private schools, including the Phillips Exeter Academy in New Hampshire and the Lawrenceville School in New Jersey.[26] Strictly speaking, the Harkness approach was designed for approximately a dozen students, who sit around an oval table and discuss the daily topic with minimal intervention by the teacher. Most public schools do not have such tables in all their classrooms, but teachers can create their equivalent by dividing up the class into two or three groups, with chairs arranged in a circle for each group. Another technique Lynn has used is a variation of the Harkness table, in which there is an inner circle of debaters and an outer circle of listeners, who critique the arguments presented in the inner circle.

Lynn has experimented with an even less intimidating way of introducing students to the claim-evidence-reasoning-counterargument-rebuttal paradigm before using the approach on "live" course material: using it on nonacademic topics first, to acquaint students with debate-style argumentation and reasoning in a nonthreatening way. As examples of possible topics to use for this exercise, he suggests such simple questions as

"Who should walk the dog this morning?"

"Is Chance the Rapper a better hip hop artist than Cardi B?"

"Is soccer [or use something else] the best sport in the world?"

Whatever the precise model teachers use at the beginning of the semester or at later points, Lynn has compiled a set of principles to govern argument-centered seminars, which are listed in the appendix to this chapter. Most of these rules apply to formal classroom debates as well.

The BDL and the teachers it assists use up to sixteen different debate-inspired techniques to drive home the "claim-evidence-reasoning" (CER) method of thinking they impart to their students. As one example, teachers arrange scavenger hunts in which students in their small group clusters are presented with teacher-prepared packets of information and then challenged to find the pieces of evidence that support specific claims. After the groups engage in this process, teachers ask the groups to present their findings to the entire class, but in an additive fashion: the first group starts, and then successive groups add other pieces of evidence to paint a broader picture. The teacher also guides discussions of the reasons why the evidence cited supports the claims, completing the CER trilogy. Lynn accepts this basic methodology but then pushes the teachers he advises and their students to go one step further, to engage in evidence-backed, reasoned arguments against certain positions taken as a way of debatifying the lessons and to train students in the art of civil discourse. Hence the "rebuttal" addition to the standard CER paradigm.

When it is time for formal debates to be used, they should probably be introduced gradually as well, perhaps by splitting the class into groups of four, with two on each side of a topic. This approach allows students to pick up debate skills without the pressure of appearing before an entire class, which they should do at some point later in the semester. In the meantime, teachers can facilitate the smaller group debate by walking around the room, monitoring, coaching, and intervening where appropriate (for example, to nip name-calling or other uncivil behavior in the bud).

Lynn cautions that, whether teachers and students are participating in argument-based seminars or in formal debates, they will not learn the fundamental techniques of debating and argumentation unless there is a clash of ideas. In other words, it is not a true debate for one speaker to state a claim backed by evidence and then for subsequent speakers to recite "canned" claims (with or without evidence) that have nothing to do with the preceding speakers' claims and evidence. The word "debate" connotes a clash between opposing claims and the presentation of whatever evidence and reasoning speakers can muster for each.

Yet another issue is whether schools interested in introducing DCI should require all their teachers to use it or support only those users who opt in. Proviso West has chosen the voluntary approach, letting each teacher in the school decide whether to participate, starting with subject matter or department chairs—approximately ten teachers of more than 100 who teach only two classes but spend the rest of their time monitoring and coaching other teachers—in the first year. The school's innovative principal, Dr. Nia Abdullah, is designing a dissemination system so that the positive experiences of the school's initial cohort of teachers using argument or DCI techniques will spread virally to other teachers. Further, Abdullah intends that at least some of the teachers in this initial cohort will train other teachers in the method, along with Lynn.[27]

The Boston schools have taken a different approach: "voluntariness" is determined at the school level. Accordingly, when the BDL partners with a school in a school-wide ACE initiative, all teachers in the school are expected to use it. All teachers in the school participate in twelve to fourteen hours of professional development training and are expected to engage in at least three coaching "cycles"—planning, classroom observation, and debriefing—for three years. Not all teachers fulfill all these requirements, but the BDL continuously works on achieving full compliance and reports increased teacher buy-in over time, especially as the success of the teachers who are most actively engaged in evidence-based argumentation is appreciated by other teachers in the schools. The BDL also piloted in the 2019–2020 academic year an opt-in "cohort" model, where a group of teachers within a school can choose to participate, which is how Lynn operates with the Chicago schools and teachers he trains and mentors.

Lynn and Wasserman and the teachers with whom they are working are not the only educators working to implement some form of DCI in public middle and high schools. Dr. Eric Tucker, who worked closely with Lynn in getting the National UDL off the ground, went on, with his wife Erin Mote, to found Brooklyn Labs charter school, which uses aspects of argument-centered instruction in its curriculum. Meagan Kowalesky, another former debater, leads New York City's famed Success Academies' efforts to offer co-curricular debate to all their students. A form of DCI is even being used for upper elementary and middle schoolers in Seattle through an organization called "DebateAble."

A number of other organizations use argument-based teaching methods as a subsidiary skill and strategy, such as the DBQ Project (www.dbqproject.com/) and the Stanford History Education Group (https://sheg.stanford.edu/). Several UDL chapters have stand-alone argumentation projects. And, as already noted, a variation of DCI, the Harkness seminars, can be found in some of the nation's elite private schools.

Some Topics Cannot and Should Not Debated

DCI is not suited for all subjects, whether in public or private school, however. Clearly, there is no room for debating or contesting well-established laws of physics or mathematics (although, as noted earlier, the claim-evidence-reasoning paradigm still can be useful in teaching math), or the existence of certain events that have been thoroughly documented by historians or archeologists: wars, incidents of ethnic cleansing, the Holocaust, or that blacks were captured in Africa and suffered grossly inhuman treatment as slaves in this country. There are not "two" sides to such matters.

Public schools are also not the place to require students to take both sides of matters of religion or faith, or subjects in which one side will take an absolutist position, claiming it is dictated by God, such as the controversial questions surrounding abortion or the origins of life, where advocates of "intelligent design" versus evolution and the theory of natural selection (the latter well established in science), simply would talk past each other. On such matters, debate has no usefulness and could be counterproductive, quickly degenerating into shouting matches. As Jay Heinrichs has written his popular book on the art of persuasion *Thank You for Arguing*: "Argument's Rule Number One: **Never debate the undebatable**"[28] (bold emphasis in the original).

None of this casts any doubt on the fact that students can and should be taught through nondebate pedagogical methods the extent to which religion has influenced the course of events through time, as part of world history. Debates, formal or informal, over the merits of one religion over another, however, do not belong in public schools (although private schools may and often do consider such matters, especially if the schools are affiliated with or operated by a religious institution).

Ultimately, the question of what subjects should be off limits in classes where DCI is used is best answered at the local level, preferably by school boards and not by individual teachers, who have enough on their plates without the added burden, or the danger to their jobs, of asking students to take both sides of certain controversial issues. Nonetheless, I believe one bright line can and should be drawn.

We live in a country defined by the shared ideal that "all men [women] are created equal, that they are endowed by their Creator with certain inalienable rights" (Declaration of Independence), and commitment to a democratic form of government constrained by the rule of law (our Constitution, statutes enacted by the Congress or state legislatures, and the "common law" generated first by Great Britain). Forms of government or beliefs that are fundamentally inconsistent with these basic principles—totalitarianism in any form (Nazism, Communism, or dictatorship) or white supremacy—should be taught as historical matters but not debated, at least in the public schools. Whether and how the United States should oppose these systems in other countries, however, are worthy subjects of debate and teaching, as are different types of democracies (the U.S. system of separation of powers vs. parliamentary systems), or theories about how and under what circumstances certain ideological viruses, such as those advocating violence or terrorism, form and take hold and how best to inoculate society against them.

Beyond the bright line test, local school boards may debate (irony intended) whether other controversial matters should be taught through debate or through conventional teaching. This includes subjects on which there is overwhelming scientific consensus but still some dispute among adults, such as the existence of man-made climate change and what should be done about it.

My own view is that public schools can ask students to debate multiple sides of these matters as a way of teaching the subjects, so long as the students understand the scientific consensus or the applicable legal precedent and its rationale on such controversial topics, but others may have a different view. Again, take the example of climate change. While there is overwhelming consensus among scientists that human activities affect the climate, and, indeed, current school curriculum standards clearly state this to be the case, there are uncertainties about the magnitude and pace of these effects, as well as what policy responses are appropriate—especially given that the actions of one city, state, or even country can only marginally affect man-made global climate change. Each of these subjects can be topics of debate-centered learning. In contrast, there are no credible scientists, to my knowledge, who believe in intelligent design rather than evolution, and thus there is no purpose to debating these contrasting topics.

I realize that just raising the question whether certain controversial matters should be open to debate can be used by some to reject the entire exercise of DCI. School boards and courts, however, have already wrestled with such questions when considering whether they belong in the classroom using conventional teacher-led instruction. Moreover, my own strong preference is that local school boards keep the number of prohibited subjects to a minimum and not use the introduction of argument- or debate-centered instruction as a means for stifling teacher creativity in the classroom.

How Early Should DCI Start?

Although the principal focus in this book is on encouraging greater use of DCI to educate high school students, DCI has its uses at both the college level (discussed shortly), in middle school, and in the later years of elementary school. Broward County's competitive debate initiative begins as early as the 4th grade. The Oracy program in Great Britain trains elementary students in closely related speaking and oral skills.[29]

Regardless of when it is introduced, students are likely to become more engaged in the *fun* of learning through DCI in a way that standard teacher-led lectures cannot be expected to deliver. Benjamin Franklin recognized this over three centuries ago when he observed: "Tell me and I forget, teach me and I may remember, *involve me and I learn*"[30] (emphasis added). There is no better way of involving students in their own learning than having them research, defend, and debate a proposition relevant to their classroom material. As one of the students in the OneStone program in Boise, Idaho, said, as cited in Dintersmith's book: "My favorite experience in school was on the debate team, because I got to learn what's going on in the world, about empathy, current events. *Nowhere else in my school experience do I get that*"[31] (emphasis added). But why limit that hugely beneficial impact of debate to an extracurricular activity?

Accordingly, the earlier in life students can be motivated to want to learn, the more they will accomplish in school and the better equipped they will be in the workforce after their initial formal schooling ends. Early introduction to DCI and the motivation for learning it provides is especially important for students from low-income families, who typically start and stay behind higher-achieving students from wealthier families attending higher-performing schools.[32]

This is not to deny the importance of early pre-K "ready-to-school" programs for such children, which Nobel-prize winning economist James Heckman has documented to be the most cost-effective of all education reforms but only if implemented through high-quality programs staffed by qualified personnel.[33] The President's Council of Economic Advisers estimated in 2014 that a dollar spent on such programs yields more than $8 in benefits to society—in terms of improved productivity and reduced crime and other social ills.[34] There are even pilot programs using the social savings as a revenue source to back the issuance of so-called "social impact bonds."[35]

But even children who benefit from early childhood education—in fact, all students—must continue to be motivated to learn as they go through school. My claim here, elaborated more fully later in this chapter and beyond, is that debate-centered education is an inexpensive and highly cost-effective way to do precisely that.

DCI is especially important in this age when too many children are addicted to their computers and smartphones at the expense of the development of their social and interpersonal skills.[36] Lukianoff and Haidt cite this tech addiction, fueled by the rise of social media, as a major reason so many students, upon arriving at college, become so brittle and fearful of any ideas or speakers who make them feel "uncomfortable." Personalized learning through innovative computer-based education platforms, while useful if coupled with effective teacher coaching, can also dull students' oral and thinking skills if not supplemented with techniques like DCI that require them to refine these skills. Requiring students to debate multiple subjects in their pre-college years forces them to look up from their screens and interact in a civil way with others. Requiring students to orally back up answers to questions opens their eyes to multiple points of view and sharpens their critical thinking, attributes that are keys to success in and out of the classroom.

DCI: Will It Work?

How can policymakers and educators know that DCI, as it has been implemented or will be implemented in the future, actually "works"—in the limited sense of enhancing student achievement, determined through the imperfect metric of test scores, through enhanced student engagement, and/or by improving the satisfaction of teachers who use DCI techniques in their classrooms? As noted, it is a fundamental reality that won't be changed in the short run that principals, teachers, and school board members are most often judged by student test scores. As long as that is the case, few of these parties are likely to adopt DCI without concrete evidence that DCI will improve student test scores, even though, for all the excellent reasons Ted Dintersmith (among others) clearly establishes, test scores are highly imperfect and may be counterproductive measures of student achievement since the continued emphasis on raising them likely turns off many students to learning.[37]

In my view, DCI is likely to meet the test score challenge, not only because it is a more effective form of pedagogy than sage on the stage lecturing but because students receiving DCI-based instruction are likely to be more motivated to learn, and increased student engagement alone should raise test scores as well as lead to more meaningful outcomes relevant to students when they reach adulthood, such as spurring creativity and stimulating a lifelong interest in learning. Engagement is important because it is related to, and for many students a prerequisite for, what psychologist Angela Duckworth calls "grit" (sticking with it) and having a "growth mindset" (not accepting that one's fate in life is fixed but, rather, believing you can improve at almost anything by putting in the work).[38] Grit is like a lightbulb waiting to be turned on by your parents, peers, or teachers. Students are more likely to want to do something and to stay with it if the activity is fun and a bit challenging. Debate-centered education provides both.

Although it has its limits, comparisons of student performance before and after DCI has been implemented provide some evidence of its positive impact. Consider these before-and-after results from Lynn's experience with argument-based instruction in the schools he has assisted over the past several years:[39]

- Two of the Chicago schools that have partnered with him have recorded substantial school-wide increases, well over 40 percent, on the reading and writing and the essay portions of the ACT.

- One of Argument-Centered Education's partner high schools improved its school-wide scores in the Evidence-Based Reading and Writing section on the SAT by 61 percent in school year 2017. Another partner high school improved its scores on the essay portion by 44 percent in that year.

- Argument-Centered Education has developed an argument-centered strategy for the essay portion of the AP Language and Composition exam (whose questions may also be a source for classroom debate topics). One partner school that has adopted this strategy in 2018 saw a 31 percent increase in student scores and a 26 percent increase in the number of students earning college credit.

- Two of the principals of schools where Lynn has worked with teachers on ACE have reported substantial improvement in teacher instructional skills and satisfaction.

Lynn's reported results are consistent with the fact that the new SAT is heavily argument-based: the dreaded analogy section of the verbal portion of the test has been replaced by questions around various reading passages that ask students to identify the "evidence" backing certain claims in the material, while the new writing test elicits essays from students designed to measure their ability to analyze written material using evidence supplied in the excerpted passages. As noted earlier in this chapter, the overhaul of the SAT was spearheaded by the president of the College Board, David Coleman, who has been a member of the board of the New York Urban Debate League.

Wasserman of the BDL reports similar improvements in the schools his organization has counseled:[40]

- Across all the BDL's partner schools, 100 percent of school principals or headmasters, and over 90 percent of teachers, reported in the school year spanning 2018–2019 that the BDL's Debate in the Classroom initiative helps students build critical thinking and argumentation skills (claim, evidence, and reasoning), improves collaboration with peers as learners, builds classroom environments in which student voice is central, and fosters high student engagement. Multiple teacher testimonials back up these survey results.

- The BDL has developed ways to measure students' argumentative writing skills within authentic assessments over the course of the school year and has found consistent substantial increases in students' ability to state claims, incorporate evidence, and communicate their reasoning.

■ As in Chicago, teachers participating in the Boston program developed by the BDL report substantial improvements in their own teaching and in their satisfaction with their jobs.

At this writing, the BDL is subjecting its argument-based learning program to more rigorous analysis by a team of researchers led by University of Virginia professor Beth Schuler. The analysis is retrospective, in that it seeks to explain through statistical methods, controlling for self-selection in ways similar to those used by Brianna Mezuk and her team when studying the impact of competitive debate on Chicago high school students, the educational impacts of argument- or evidence-based instruction on middle and high school students who have already been instructed through those methods.

For reasons elaborated on in the first two chapters, DCI instruction in the future ideally should be evaluated through one or more randomized control trials (RCTs), which should cover multiple subjects taught in high school and middle school. Also, ideally, students (and teachers) should be followed for extensive periods of time after school to test the impacts of the instructional technique on workplace outcomes, the willingness of students to retrain, and impacts on their civic and political behavior (all for reasons that will become obvious in the next two chapters).

The absence of an RCT rigorously confirming the educational and other benefits of DCI, however, needn't and shouldn't stand in the way of further experimentation with this method of instruction. If the retrospective study by Shuler confirms the before-after experiences that Lynn and the BDL have already shown in Chicago and Boston, that may be enough to encourage implementation of DCI in other school districts. Hopefully, the simple logic behind the idea will motivate entrepreneurial schools and school districts—especially those already experimenting with project based-learning—to include DCI as a component in their instruction. In fact, at this writing, a major evaluation is underway by researchers at the University of Southern California of an RCT of PBL implemented in five of the largest metropolitan school districts in the country: Boston, Charlotte, Chicago, Fairfax County outside of Washington, D.C., and Los Angeles. Since PBL is a close instructional cousin to DCI, the outcome of that evaluation should shed some light on the educational benefits of the latter.

There are at least three reasons debate-centered education should improve educational performance and teacher satisfaction. One is that the process of preparing for debate, knowing how to research, and then actually doing it, is perhaps the ultimate form of "active learning," in which students engage in learning directly rather than passively sitting through lectures and sometimes taking notes (imperfectly). Just as you are more likely to remember something if you write it down than type it up on a word processor on a tablet or personal computer, you are more likely to remember and think critically if you are engaged in teaching yourself and others about a given subject, provided you also have a coach or mentor—namely, the teacher, overseeing or assessing your work. That is precisely what debate-centered education does.

Admittedly, DCI may not be as effective as lecture-based learning at the very beginning of a semester, when students have little or no familiarity with the subject matter of the class—although a case can be made that using debate at the outset is a good way to excite students. In any event, after a few weeks, when students have gotten the hang of the material being taught—whether it is English, history, civics, or even some scientific topics—they should have the ability to research new topics, with the guidance of the teacher.

Indeed, with the internet, students can discover much beyond any assigned initial reading —perhaps too much, and the wrong things, as discussed in chapter 6's coverage of the "debate over truth." This is a problem, but not an unsurmountable one, to implementing DCI.

A second reason DCI is likely to be effective, for students and teachers alike, is that it is fun, and for that reason alone it should engage students in the joy of learning for its own sake, not just to pass a test or complete a course of study. Most students, especially at middle and high school ages, want to express themselves in some way. Debate offers a way for them to do that in a constructive fashion, one that demonstrates the importance of learning while equipping those students with skills they can use in their personal, professional, and civic lives well after their formal schooling ends.

Debate-centered education, at least for some students, may also act as a "gateway" toward competitive debate, which is likely to have even greater educational advantages than DCI. As it is now, only certain students may know about competitive debate, from their older siblings or a parent, or perhaps their peers. Once they are learning through debate methods, many more may realize they would be good competitive debaters. The story of Brian Hufford told in the first chapter—who was taught through debate-centered techniques in middle school in Dodge City Kansas forty years ago, became involved in competitive debate, and ultimately turned out to a highly successful trial lawyer—is an example of how this positive "gateway effect" can work.

To be sure, there is one potential downside of debate-centered education for some students—doing poorly. Not just at first, which is likely to be common for those with little public speaking experience, but consistently not improving for any number of reasons. The shame from this kind of failure could reduce some students' interest in learning and, perhaps, negatively affect their personal lives.

The risk and fact of failure already exists with written examinations, however. Students with poor grades, understandably, are at risk of continuing to do poorly in school and of dropping out altogether. Debate-centered activities are no different in this respect, although they have more immediate and public consequences. Some students, like athletes who make a mistake or fail on the field or on the court, may react to public failure by vowing to do better out of the fear of further embarrassment or a competitive desire to do better next time. They learn that failure is part of life and that learning how to overcome failure and mistakes is one of life's most important lessons.

Of course, failure for some students could produce a vicious cycle of failure, which is why teachers delivering DCI should be prepared to mentor and tutor lagging students to buck them up and show them how to succeed. Breaking out students of different abilities into different subgroups is a way to anticipate this problem and minimize the numbers of students who suffer loss of confidence and self-esteem in the process. Ideally, all students will gain, though to varying degrees, from DCI, but if some don't, despite the best efforts of targeted counseling, the "fear of failing a few" should not be a reason to deprive the vast majority of students of the benefits that DCI can deliver.

Debate-Centered Instruction and Three Targeted Student Groups

Not only would debate-centered education broadly improve interest in learning and educational performance, but there are good reasons for believing that it would also help address the special challenges of the three student groups identified at the outset of this chapter.

Students from Disadvantaged Backgrounds

Begin with students from low-income backgrounds, often from broken homes and neighborhoods in the inner city. Up to now, the most promising way out for a select few is to be randomly assigned to an eagerly sought-after, high quality charter school or a high quality "magnet" public school. The rest, surely the vast majority of students who from the day they start school are already behind, are left to fend for themselves in poorly performing local neighborhood schools, where despite the best efforts of good teachers, peer pressure to join gangs or not to "act white" can overwhelm the desire of even the brightest students with the best of intentions to apply themselves to learning on a sustained basis.

The key to overcoming these hurdles is to find ways of engaging students in the joy or fun of learning. Students from upper income families with high expectations for their children, coupled with resources devoted to their learning and outside-of-school lessons, summer camps and the like, have built-in advantages in overcoming the chores and stresses of the classroom. Children from families without these advantages are lucky to survive the education gauntlet. Telling them they must succeed in school so they can get into and complete college—an eternity away to youth who may be risking their lives just walking home from school—and have a successful life thereafter can easily fall on deaf ears, especially if students are without role models to follow. The standard lecture format of teaching may not be helpful either. As Proviso West's principal, Dr. Nia Abdullah, put it to me: sage on the stage teaching can easily lead to student boredom, which in turn leads to some students acting out, disrupting the class, and thus ruining the educational experience for their peers. Debate or argument-centered instruction, in her view, is one important way of making the classroom experience relevant to students' daily lives while actively engaging them in learning, not simply asking them to write down and then memorize what teachers tell them.

Only if education itself is enjoyable, engaging students' desire for self-expression or appealing to their competitive instincts, can students who come to school already several steps behind have a real chance at overcoming the many obstacles that stand in their way. Some schools and some remarkable teachers may give them that chance, but this is an unsystematic process. If implemented by teachers committed to make it work, consistent application of debate-centered education—for the multiple reasons already discussed—can also make the fun and challenge routine aspects of learning, and for this reason it should be especially important for students from disadvantaged backgrounds.

Opening the eyes of such students to the joy of learning and an understanding of how it can lead to a better life will create new pathways of success. One of those roads is competitive debate. Organizations like the Matthew Orenstein Summer Debate Camp in Washington, D.C., which now trains predominantly minority students in middle and high schools from the inner city in competitive debating techniques, will find greatly enlarged demand for their services as debate becomes more routinely embedded in regular classrooms. It is no wonder. As one of the founders of the camp, AEI political scientist Norman Ornstein, observes about the camp:

I believe in equal opportunity. But it is not equal opportunity when some people start at the starting blocks, others start 20 yards behind and yet others 20 yards ahead. The Orenstein camp, and the teams that follow during the school year, are designed to teach kids skills for life.

Learning to speak in front of others, to do research, to argue all sides in a vigorous but civil fashion, to learn deep substance, all can move kids closer to the starting blocks. Watching these kids take to debate, develop self-confidence and thrive is simply thrilling.

So far, we have had terrific success, our debaters getting into good colleges and doing well. The 2017 winner of the Matthew Harris Ornstein Award for the debater best exemplifying his values, Jonathan Collins of DuVal HS, was named by National Debater of the Year by the National Association for Urban Debate Leagues that year.[41]

The Ornstein summer camp's session in 2019 included a simulation of the Democratic presidential debates. While those debates are not that similar to the kind of consistent and persistent debate instruction in the classroom advocated for throughout this book, they nonetheless can engage young people in debate activities in a very direct and personal way. The camp's activities in this regard were featured in a *New York Times* article that summer.[42]

Expanded philanthropic support from foundations and caring individuals with experience and interest in education and expanding life opportunities will be required to meet this growing demand for the Orenstein camp and others like it. It may not exist now, but it will in the future, as will training programs for teachers in DCI techniques and formal evaluations of their students. This is not unrealistic. As already noted, philanthropies have played a major role in supporting a variety of educational reforms and interventions in the past and will continue to do so. One of the objectives of this book is to put DCI on their funding agendas.

Debate as Preparation for College and in College

DCI also would address the "fragility" of some of our best and brightest high school students, which Lukianoff and Haidt argue contributes to their defensiveness and unwillingness to tolerate robust debates of ideas, in and out of the classroom, once they get to college. As stated in the recommendations section of their book *The Coddling of the American Mind*:[43]

> A great way for students to learn the skills of civil disagreement is by participating in structured, formal debates. *It is especially important that students practice arguing for positions that oppose their own views.* All students would benefit from learning debating techniques and participating in formal debates. In addition to the obvious benefits of learning how to make a well-supported case, debate helps students distinguish between a critique of ideas and a personal attack (emphasis added).

These comments also raise a natural question: While middle and high schools are considering the implementation of or experimenting with DCI, a process that easily could take a decade or more, might there be value in colleges using these techniques in their classrooms, even if virtually all their students have had no prior formal debate training? One former debater, now a college professor, Richard Mercandante, made precisely this suggestion as early as 1988, arguing that one version of competitive college debate should be used in all "liberal arts" classrooms.[44]

But his idea seemed to be aimed at having students participate in a single formal debate, presumably at the end of the semester, and he was not suggesting that debate techniques be used throughout the class as a mode of instruction to supplement lecture-based learning. Ruth Kennedy has outlined several ways debate techniques can be introduced in a college setting,[45] and various websites suggest how this can be done and what topics might be debated.[46] Ted Dintersmith, in his book, reports that a distinguished physicist at Harvard uses debate techniques in his classes now, after finding that even his elite Harvard students who did well in his lecture-based classes had a poor understanding of the way physics concepts worked in the real world.[47] Diana Carlin, mentioned earlier, has taught freshman honors seminars at Kansas University using techniques she used earlier as a high school teacher.

The limited studies or reports of debate instructional techniques used in college classes are uniformly positive. One small-scale study published in 2015 of sixteen students in a Malaysian university that used a different debate format—British Parliamentary Debate—reports qualitatively what one would expect debate participation to produce: more open-mindedness and better critical thinking among the students.[48] Other qualitative assessments have reported similar positive student results from the use of debate in a sophomore level English class,[49] an undergraduate class in political science,[50] a college course on technology and science,[51] and a senior level business school marketing class in the United States.[52] Debate techniques also have been used in professional schools, nursing in Ireland for example, [53] and through the Socratic method used in most law schools and in some business schools. One study of the use of debate in the college classroom in Singapore found high levels of teacher satisfaction as well as positive student assessments.[54] Admittedly, there may be a selection-bias in such studies, since authors are less likely to write, and journals less likely to publish, assessments or studies with zero or negative effects. Nonetheless, the cumulative weight of these one-off publications at the very least establishes what lawyers would call a *prima facie* case for the value of DCI at the college level and even beyond.

One practical question arises: Should colleges encourage more of these experiments with instructors willing to use debate techniques in their classes, or should something more systematic be tried? Clearly,

I believe the latter approach is preferable. If Lukianoff and Haidt are right that too many college students today arrive on campus unable to tolerate critical debate—an attitude that probably is amplified by the contacts and friendships they make once they are there—then waiting for the random professor to incorporate DCI in his or her class at some point in the four-year college program may be too late. Why shouldn't colleges devote at least a portion of the pre-registration week for incoming freshman to instruction in basic debate techniques (perhaps students with competitive debate experience or who come from high schools where they have received DCI may be exempted from this requirement)? Ideally, this introduction to debate would be supplemented by having some form of DCI incorporated in at least one or two subjects freshmen take during their first semester, so that all students are familiarized from the beginning of their college experience in the ways of conducting civil discourse and argument with each other, with a wide range of ideas, and with their teachers. In large lecture classes, DCI instruction logistically would have to be implemented in the breakout sessions that typically accompany the lectures.

Colleges may have the same challenges of convincing their professors to buy in to DCI instructional techniques, as many middle and high schools confront with their teachers. Indeed, resistance at the college level could be greater given that some professors who have first-year classes may be popular, tenured, and already well set in their ways. One way around this is to convince professors in large lecture courses to have their teaching assistants use DCI in break-out sessions as a way of reinforcing or clarifying issues raised in the lectures. This would entail some modest additional training cost for TAs, which would have the side benefit of developing their expertise in DCI at the outset of their careers, which would likely change the way many of them teach once they have earned their Ph.Ds.

DCI at the college level, or ideally before, would have one other benefit. As a counterreaction to the intolerance for the free debate of ideas on college campuses, in March 2019, President Trump issued an Executive Order tying federal research grants to whether, in the judgment of federal officials, universities are complying with the First Amendment. This is a troublesome development, for it poses the danger of political interference in research functions, and it could cost universities important federal support and disrupt the research activities of professors who have no control over whether their university-employers are complying with a free speech code in the abstract or, more concretely, are complying with the views of federal officials about such compliance. It would be far better to encourage student open-mindedness through exposure to DCI than to have the heavy and potentially biased hand of government on the shoulder of our nation's research institutions.

Female Students

DCI could be especially valuable for girls. Even as they have outperformed boys in school for some years—to the point where numerous books and articles have attempted to answer the question "What's the matter with boys?"—it is still widely recognized that girls speak up in class and in the workplace less frequently than boys.[55] This is the case even though girls develop language skills earlier than boys.[56]

The study by Briana Mezuk and her colleagues discussed in chapter 2 demonstrated that more girls than boys participated in competitive debate in Chicago and, thus, collectively benefitted more than boys from that activity. That experience augurs well for girls responding in a constructive way to the introduction of DCI throughout the school curriculum, giving them the confidence to speak up at a relatively early age and to carry that confidence into the workplace and into the rest of their lives. In the process, DCI could change cultural attitudes of boys at an early age and, thus, help equalize the workplace and eventually help make Sheryl Sandberg's "lean in" advice for girls and women obsolete.

Ironically, China, a country without democracy, has been experimenting with debate in education, where girls especially have excelled.[57] Surely, the United States, the world's leading democracy, should be able to match that experience.

DCI Is Part of the Next Revolution in Education

For decades, various authors have expressed the need to shift the lecture-based educational model, which was well suited to provide basic skills for the industrial age, to a more customized system tailored to the needs and abilities of individual students. Customized instruction is available today in exclusive private schools but, with some exceptions, has not scaled well to public school environments nor to the need today to give students an augmented set of basic skills (such as the ability to code) and to motivate them to want to continue improving and updating their skills for a rapidly changing, increasingly automated workplace.

Computerized learning systems, such as the short videos developed by the Khan Academy, satisfy the need to tailor lecture-based learning to the different abilities of different students, but they are still based on the lecture model. Exercises accompanying software instruction help students understand the material, and the ability to chat with teachers on other online educational platforms provides some interactivity and, thus, an additional element of customization. But even these cutting-edge pedagogical tools do not fundamentally change the instructor-led model of learning.

DCI is a fundamental change in pedagogy. It puts much more of the onus on learning on individual students, with guidance and mentorship of the teacher, plus feedback and interactivity with peers. DCI also can take advantage of the massive amount of researchable information available on the internet today by requiring students to find it, sort through it, and, with guidance, determine what is reliable and what is not.

But most important, DCI instills and refines critical thinking skills of students while encouraging open-mindedness by requiring students to take both or (possibly) more sides of contested issues or topics. DCI, thus, engages students in teaching themselves, with the assistance of teachers, a process that should enable students to retain information they uncover themselves and encourage them to be inquisitive throughout their lives in the constant search for truth.

All of this should be good for students in school and the workplace and have important and positive effects on our collective political life. That important subject is addressed in the next chapter.

APPENDIX 3-A

Rules for Argument-Based Seminars (Addressed to Students)

You should speak at least twice.

There are four—and only four—things you can do in an argument-based seminar: make an argument, respond to or refute another argument, evaluate clashing arguments, or ask a question. Strive to make at least one argument and respond to at least one critique.

Every time you speak, you should reference evidence.

Every time you speak, you should add something new to the discussion.

Understand that the purpose of argumentation in a seminar is insight and learning, not winning.

Always align your contributions to the debatable question(s).

Reason through the importance (the "so what?") of your claim and evidence.

Track or take notes on the arguments made during the seminar.

When responding to an argument, summarize the argument first.

You should try to defend your position, but you can change your mind.

Source: Les Lynn, Argument-Centered Education (provided to the author).

FOUR

Debate-Centered Instruction Can Help Revitalize Our Democracy

How, then, do we live together in this world of differing ideas? For starters, let's agree that the ideas are fair game. If you think my idea is awful, you should say as much. But there is a difference between attacking an idea and attacking the person behind that idea.

Congressman Dan Crenshaw (R-TX) (2018)[1]

When events change, I change my mind. What do you do?

Paul Samuelson, Economist and Nobel Laureate (1970)[2]

The following thought experiment was one reason I was driven to write this book. Imagine that every American citizen had some debate training in middle or high school, of the type outlined in the previous chapter. By this, I mean that all citizens, in their formal education, learn to argue persuasively, using facts and reason, in a civil manner about a variety of issues. Most important, they learn to advocate effectively for both or multiple sides of virtually any topic, with the exceptions identified in chapter 3. If these conditions held, do you think our polity would be as polarized—or more accurately, tribal—as it has become?

To me, the answer is clear: "Of course not." You may already be convinced of this after reading the previous chapters, but in case you're not, this chapter makes the case for why having more students—all of them, ideally—instructed in debate-centered techniques during at least some of their formal schooling would help heal our political divisions and improve the functioning of our democracy. This may happen gradually, of course, but would be a positive outcome that ought to be welcome nonetheless.

I do not claim that the sources of division in our country—economic, cultural, religious, or racial—would be any less intense. Rather, my claim is that many, perhaps most, of us would *react differently* to these underlying differences and be more tolerant of them, perhaps even celebrate them or recognize that the diversity of backgrounds and experiences across our country is a strength and not a weakness. These attitudinal shifts will be especially important during the coming decades as the non-Hispanic share of whites continues to fall, a multi-decade trend dating from the end of World War II that is expected to lower the white population to less than 50 percent by sometime in the middle of the twenty-first century.[3] Awareness of this prospect is fueling the sharp rise in hate crimes in America, and even some mass shootings.

These claims, which are centered on the potential ability of debate-centered instruction to narrow our tribal divisions, are based on logic and statements or inferences drawn from many of the former debaters interviewed for this book as well as my own debating experience in high school and college. It is doubtful that any single one or group of foundations or philanthropists will any time soon underwrite a randomized control trial spanning the ten or twenty years or more that would be required to follow treatment and control groups of students in different schools or school districts who are given the kind of debate training in middle and high school described in earlier chapters to test the foregoing conclusion and additional propositions advanced in this chapter. But for the reasons given here, I am confident that such a study would reach many, if not all, of the conclusions that follow.

Thoughtful Debate Is Essential
to a Healthy Democracy

Look up "debate" on the web (or in a hard-copy dictionary) and you'll find two basic definitions, depending on whether the word is used as a noun or a verb.[4] When used as a noun, the term refers to a "formal discussion on a particular topic in a public meeting or legislative assembly, in which *opposing* arguments are put forward" (emphasis added). As a verb, the term means to "argue about [a subject], *especially in a formal manner*" (emphasis added). The italicized phrases in the two definitions identify a fundamental characteristic of debate central to the theme of this book: the ability to discuss formally, but in a civil way, multiple sides of any topic is a skill that can be learned and, once learned, confers substantial benefits to individuals and society.

Typically, autocrats, dictators, and kings, and probably too many (poor) chief executive officers of companies have no use for debate. They don't want opposing views or dissent in their inner ranks or in the populaces they govern or the workplaces they oversee. History shows this to be a great flaw, because all leaders, no matter how powerful, can benefit from not only hearing diverse viewpoints but having them actively debated before them.

Democracies, at least in principle, do not suffer this problem. To the contrary, elected leaders of democratically governed countries operate with the consent of voters (unless the voters are so rash and disillusioned as to surrender their power to an autocrat, as the Germans did with Hitler), and they or their appointees must debate what to do about a myriad of policy issues, both in the open and behind closed doors, with their advisers, cabinet-level officials, and members of the legislature. Likewise, appellate courts, including the Supreme Court, listen to legal debates by attorneys from both sides, and once they adjourn to deliberate, debate among themselves, sometimes orally though more frequently through exchanges of memoranda and draft opinions. As commentator Van Jones writes in his thoughtful book *Beyond the Messy Truth*: "Debate is the lifeblood of democracy, after all. Disagreement is a good thing—even heated disagreement. Only in a dictatorship does everyone have to agree."[5]

Likewise, in a speech exploring the contributions of the great University of Chicago economist Frank Knight, Ross Emmett of Arizona State credits Knight with this pithy summary: "Democratic action [is] essentially government by discussion."[6] Debate is nothing more than structured, civil discussion.

Debates, by definition, presuppose at least two sides to any issue or question. Shouting matches, often full of ad hominem attacks of the kind we see routinely on cable television, also have two sides. But these "debates" are meant to entertain, agitate, or validate the views observers already hold. In contrast, debates that focus on substance, ideally structured with time limits for each side and without name-calling, are constructive for at least two reasons.

First, healthy debate compels the participants—the debaters themselves—to sharpen their arguments, which is useful to them in shaping their own thoughts, and if they are in positions of power, also useful in identifying ways opposing sides may be able to reach consensus or compromise. In performing this function, debates that start out with two opposing sides can facilitate agreement somewhere in the middle.

Second, debates generally presuppose an audience, whom the debaters address and attempt to persuade. In a democracy, voters are the audience. Good debates, by bringing out the best arguments for any given proposition, while also exposing weaknesses and fallacies, perform a valuable educational function for those listening, enabling them, at least in principle, to make more informed choices when voting. Indeed, a major reason we educate our children, apart from readying them for the workforce, is to equip them with critical thinking ability, along with knowledge of our history and that of other countries, and the workings of democracy so that when they become adults they will become good citizens.

Central to good citizenship, and indeed to having a successful career and family and being happy about it, is having an open mind, one that is capable of being changed when evidence and logic warrant it. Humans and all organizations are constantly learning and adapting to changes, whether foreseen or unforeseen. Science proceeds by constant formulation and testing of hypotheses, a process that clearly requires being receptive to evidence and facts. Likewise, businesses are constantly getting feedback—in the form of sales and profits—on how well their products and services are being accepted in the marketplace. Businesses that don't adapt to those signals will die. Even successful businesses won't grow without developing new products and services, typically a process of trial and error and one that depends on continuous feedback from purchasers.

What is true for individuals and businesses also holds for government, although the process of collective decisionmaking is typically slower and frequently less rational than in the private sector. There are many reasons for this, among them that performance measures for societies or polities may not be widely agreed upon and because different interests affect what is decided. Ignoring facts and evidence also doesn't help. Law professor Peter Schuck has written clearly and authoritatively about how these factors and others have contributed to acrimony in our politics, and how they make it difficult for the U.S. democratic system to tackle "hard" issues.[7] Still, as imperfect as it is, democracies will produce more widely accepted results over time than autocracies. And, in a democracy, when enough voters at least believe or perceive that their leaders are not performing as expected, they will vote them out and replace them with others.

In short, learning by individuals and organizations, by definition, can't happen unless people are open to understanding and incorporating new information, facts, or theories and, if appropriate, doing things differently, often changing their minds in the process. As argued in the last chapter, debating in school at a relatively early age offers one of the best ways to learn and retain what you learn while developing the mindset that enables you to react more promptly and with greater wisdom to constantly changing facts, whether they affect your private life, your work or business, or your political attitudes.

Open Minds, Compromise, and Democracy

An open mind does not mean an empty one. We all need mental frameworks or philosophies to provide a context or mental structure for sorting and understanding facts, whether in our private lives and on the infrequent (or frequent, for some of us) occasions when we think about government and political issues. Many put much greater trust in the operation of markets, the combined outcomes determined by buyers and sellers of goods and services, than they do in government. Others have greater faith in collective decisions, or government, to guide, soften, or replace market-determined outcomes. The mental frameworks of some in both camps (or those who are agnostic between the two) are guided or based largely on their religion. Academic scholars continue to debate how and where our mental frameworks come from: through our genetic makeup, our environment, or some combination of the two.

Regardless of origin, democracy works best when our mental frameworks are not so rigid that we become blind to facts that call for adapting or rethinking them. I am confident, for example, that many more Americans became more concerned about terrorist threats after the awful events of 9/11. Likewise, many Americans had their faith in government, in markets, or in both, shaken by the financial crisis of 2008 and the deep recession that followed it. Whether we like it or not, we are confronted with constant change—due to technological innovations, changes in social mores, wars, and other unforeseen events—inside and outside our borders. Having a mental framework helps us understand and respond to these changes, but we must also be open to the possibility that our frameworks don't dictate all the answers or that they are insufficient by themselves to supply them, and there may be a need to change the frameworks we have now, or even develop new ones. Judges, especially those on the Supreme Court, are faced with this daunting task, perhaps more so in the coming years.[8] Legislators and businesses must face the need to adapt to new facts and circumstances, and so must each of us in our working lives (the subject of the next chapter).

In all of these contexts, we will be better able to adapt to change if we are also able to compromise, a feature central in any well-functioning organization or government. In the political realm, the importance of compromise is underscored by the experience of a political figure known much better in Europe than in the United States, Alexis Tsipras, who was elected prime minister of Greece in 2015. Tsipras ran on what many characterized at the time as an ideologically nationalistic platform vigorously opposing the conditions the International Monetary Fund and European governments imposed on continued lending to his country. Eventually Tsipras accepted those terms (though it cost him his leadership position), later saying: "We are a party [Syriza] that belongs to the European family of the *governing* left. *And if you govern, you have to make compromises*" (emphasis added).[9] American readers take note: this is a politician in *Greece* underscoring the importance of compromise.

Of course, Americans shouldn't have to take lessons from Greece, or anywhere else for that matter, since compromise is built into the U.S. Constitution, which itself was the product of a series of compromises aimed at enlisting the support of all thirteen colonies. Alexander Hamilton wanted the new federal government to assume the debts of all states, with twin purposes: to unify the nation and to establish a liquid market in the debt of the entire country. To meet the objection of the southern states, which viewed the federal assumption of the states' debt as a bailout of the more heavily indebted northern states, Hamilton agreed to move the nation's capital from Philadelphia to a more southern location, Washington, D.C. A similar north-south split led to a more infamous compromise over apportioning congressional representatives across the states. Since slaves couldn't vote, ignoring their numbers, as the North initially wanted, would have given Northern states more congressional seats than the South's initial position, which was to count slaves fully in apportioning congressional representatives in the House. Eventually, the Constitutional Convention compromised on an idea originally floated by James Madison in earlier debates over how to revise the Articles of Confederation in order to

collect taxes by counting slaves as 3/5 of a "person,"[10] a noxious provi-
sion that remained in the Constitution until after the Civil War, when
the Fourteenth Amendment, ratified in 1868, granted equal rights to all
Americans, including former slaves.

The Constitution also constructed a system of multi-layered checks
and balances—of the three formal branches of government on each
other and, through the First Amendment, the protection of a free press
to serve as a check on all three governmental branches—that inherently compels compromise on a continuing basis. I am not a historian
and, thus, cannot recite the many examples throughout our history
where compromises were essential for legislation to be enacted. But I
can single out a few examples from my own lifetime that amply prove
the point.

Civil rights legislation prohibiting discrimination against blacks,
and later against women and the disabled, would not have been possible
without some bipartisan support. The major elements of the modern
safety net—Social Security, Medicare, and Medicaid—while advocated
principally by Democrats, also were and have been supported by many
Republicans. Laws protecting safety in the workplace and the environment were championed by a Republican president (Nixon) and supported by members of both political parties in Congress.

Compromises were and remain especially necessary when the two
branches of government are controlled by different parties. Think of
the bipartisan legislation enacted during the Reagan administration
in 1983 that fortified (for at least several decades) the finances of the
Social Security system and the remarkable 1986 Tax Reform Act, which
used the added revenues from closing tax loopholes (broadening the
"tax base") to substantially lower marginal tax rates across the income
scale. Or the Americans for Disabilities Act and the deficit reduction
legislation that married caps on spending with higher taxes during the
George H. W. Bush administration (Bush's courageous support of the
tax provisions probably cost him reelection). Likewise, Bill Clinton "tri-
angulated" bipartisan backing for both welfare reform and his deficit
reduction package during his second term. Even Republican president

George W. Bush, who pushed through major tax cuts like President Reagan before him, almost entirely on a partisan basis, worked with Democrats to enact the No Child Left Behind education reform bill (whose major features have since been largely reversed), expansion of Medicare coverage for prescription drugs, and, perhaps most famously (or infamously, depending on your perspective), the "bailout" legislation that helped rescue the financial system from collapsing during the financial crisis of fall 2008.

The Rise of Political Polarization

In our times of partisan political strife, it may come as a surprise to some readers that the Constitution makes no mention of "political parties"—groups of citizens who hold common views or have common interests about how government should operate—nor did all of the "founding founders" envision that permanent parties would emerge. Our first president, George Washington, was not affiliated with any political party and even condemned them. In his farewell (written) address to the nation in 1796, Washington warned that parties were the "worst enemy" of government, "agitating the community with ill-founded jealousies and false alarms," which would set "the animosity of one part against the other," perhaps leading to "riot and insurrection."[11] James Madison, in *Federalist Paper No. 10*, also warned that the multiplication of "factions"—"a number of citizens, whether amounting to a majority or minority of the whole, who are united and actuated by some common impulse of passion, or of interest, adverse to the rights of other citizens, or to the permanent and aggregate interests of the community"—could make democracy dysfunctional.[12] Likewise, Presidents John Adams and his son John Quincy Adams both disdained partisan alignments.[13]

Summing all this up, historian Gordon Wood has written that the earliest political parties that emerged following Washington's presidency, the Federalists and the Republicans, "were not modern parties" in the sense we know them today, and that *"No one* thought the emergence of parties was a good thing; indeed, far from building a party system in the 1790s, the nation's leaders struggled to prevent one from happening."[14]

To state the obvious now, that is not the way things have turned out. Parties have become central features of American political life. They have also reflected fundamental philosophical differences over the way the nation should be governed. The division between the Federalists who advocated a strong national or centralized government and early Republicans who favored decentralized power has continued to this day.

Although two parties have been dominant at any one time throughout U.S. history, they have not been ideologically pure, which is to say that not every party member always has subscribed to the same views on all issues. But this heterogeneity has served the nation well and allowed government to function. When members of each party can cross "the aisle" to support versions of what the other party wants, compromise is more likely.

Unfortunately, compromise today has become the equivalent of a four-letter word. Too many Americans have let their personas become so tightly defined by their political party that they have effectively outsourced their mental frameworks as they relate to politics and government to party leaders, making party affiliations sources of increasing division.

The political, or more accurately tribal, divisions in the electorate are reflected in the dysfunction in Washington, where elected officials in the two parties today have become more reluctant to buck congressional leaders or the president (as the case may be) from their own party. As a result, major legislation has been enacted only when one party has controlled the Executive branch and both chambers of Congress, and then only in the context of a real (or manufactured) crisis. It has become a rare occasion when a member of Congress or senator of either party has crossed over the aisle to support a member on the other side. Politicians themselves don't routinely socialize, as they once did, with members of the other party—with the rare exception of funerals.

It is difficult to pinpoint the exact time and place when this vicious cycle of partisanship began, but historian Michael Tomasky argues that it started soon after the two parties, the Federalists and the Republicans, were formed, has been as vicious in earlier periods as it is now, and has been part and parcel of our politics ever since. True, there was a relatively brief period of several decades, until President Nixon and the Watergate scandal, when there was bipartisan consensus on at least some issues—foreign policy, for example—but Tomasky views this as the exception, not the rule, and resulting from the shared scars of a generation that lived through the Great Depression and then united to fight World War II. As those common experiences wore off, so did any semblance of partisan goodwill.[15]

Whether or not Tomasky is right about the intensity of party conflict throughout the rest of our history, there is little doubt that the period since the early 1970s has spiraled toward ever greater and more intense partisanship, as reflected in the Watergate affair and President Nixon's subsequent resignation, the nomination hearings for Justice Clarence Thomas, the rise of Newt Gingrich to House Speaker and his take-no-prisoners political approach to that job, and the impeachment (but not conviction) of President Bill Clinton. Polarization was very much on display throughout the Obama presidency, which Republicans strongly opposed, and then throughout the Trump administration, including as part of his impeachment but failed conviction. As briefly noted in the opening chapter, political polarization has increased more rapidly over the past four decades in the U.S. than in other industrialized countries.[16]

Social scientists surely will argue for years about why this has happened. While they do, they would do well to keep in mind the Nobel prize–winning research of psychologist Daniel Kahneman and his late colleague Amos Tversky. These scholars identify two modes of thought that govern human behavior: "system 1" thinking, which is quick and intuitively reactive, analogous to the "fight or flight" syndrome when one is threatened, and "system 2" thinking that is "slow" and deliberative, more reasoned and rational. Kahneman, like most political scientists I have read, cautions that most people, when they vote, are in system 1 mode rather than in system 2. Jonathan Haidt, a psychologist at New York University, offers a similar distinction, using the analogy of an elephant, representing human emotions, and its rider, symbolizing rationality and reason.[17] He, too, claims that most political behavior is governed by our elephants, not by our "riding" selves. The distinctions outlined by Kahneman and Haidt essentially restate, in different terminology, the division between "reason" and "passion" found in the writings of many political economists of the nineteenth century and in numerous works of literature over the past several centuries.

Writing with Greg Lukianoff in their book *The Coddling of the American Mind*, Haidt argues that humans are hardwired to belong to groups or "tribes."[18] In the pre-modern era, hunters and gatherers relied on each other to find and share food. As history marched on, people identified with each other based on geography and, later, religion. In any event, once the "tribal switch" is activated, people can too easily quit thinking: they follow their elephants, or use system 1, ignoring the rider and system 2. Knowing the party of a candidate, or his or her philosophical label (conservative or liberal), from a TV or social media ad can stimulate the kind of automatic pattern recognition response that tells most voters all they need to know. As the highly respected historian Jon Meacham wrote about the state of U.S. politics in 2019: "We tend to assess events not in the light of reason but with the flames of partisan passion. What we make of a given moment is governed less by the merits and details and more by demands of our particular political tribe."[19]

Social media aggravate political polarization by putting us into "preference bubbles," where we tend to hear political views from our friends, family, and others we "follow" who share and reinforce our views. Roger McNamee, one of the early investors in Facebook, sums up the problem:

> Preference bubbles can be all-encompassing, especially if the platform like Facebook or Google amplifies them with a steady

diet of reinforcing content . . . In a preference bubble, users create an alternative reality, built around values shared with a tribe, which focus on politics, religion or something else. They stop interacting with people with whom they disagree, reinforcing the power of the bubble. . . . They disregard expertise in favor of voices from their tribe. They refuse to accept uncomfortable facts, even ones that are incontrovertible.[20]

The Dangers of Tribalism

Political extremism, which is both a cause and a product of political polarization, is not healthy for democracy, or for that matter, any group decisionmaking process. There is no point arguing or even attempting to engage with someone who has staked out an extreme position and sticks to it regardless of facts or reasoning that may be inconsistent with or that counterbalance it. Once people are in their political or ideological corners, there is no way to move forward or reach a compromise. That is where we find ourselves today, and it tears at the fabric of our country in several ways.

First, the rise of extremism on both sides of the political aisle, and the increased polarization of the electorate that comes with it, makes government decisions more volatile. When control of government changes, the losing party makes it a high priority to reverse what came before. This, in turn, makes it more difficult for businesses and individuals to make long-term plans.

For example, in 2010, during President Obama's first term, Democrats in Congress were able to push through on a straight party line vote the Dodd-Frank Act, meant to reduce the likelihood and severity of future financial crises, and what has come to be known as Obamacare. Given the active and uniform opposition of Republican elected officials to both acts, it was, thus, predictable that when Donald Trump won the presidency and Republicans took control over both congressional chambers in 2016, the reversal of both acts became top priorities for the first congressional term that followed. As it turned out, Republicans were more successful cutting back Dodd-Frank by legislation and regulatory action, actions that had some moderate Democratic support as well, than they have been so far with Obamacare. Nonetheless, the Trump administration has taken various executive actions to frustrate implementation of the health insurance law, while backing a broad judicial challenge to it in the lower federal courts, which at the time of this writing had reached the Supreme Court, from which a decision will not be forthcoming until after the 2020 elections.

Likewise, when Barack Obama took office, he and his fellow Democrats backed legislation that partially reversed the two tax cuts enacted during the prior Bush administration. Here, too, Republicans, when they returned to power in 2016, were able to more than reverse the Obama tax increases on upper income households in tax cut legislation enacted in 2017.

This revenge cycle of policymaking could get worse if, as many expect, the Senate eliminates the long-standing filibuster rule, which requires the approval of sixty senators before most substantive legislative proposals can be considered by the full body. (There have been an increasing number of exemptions from the sixty-vote requirement, including votes on administration appointments, most importantly judges, and budget reconciliation bills that can include almost any tax and spending legislation.) A super-majority voting requirement makes enactment of legislation and, hence, change more difficult. Conversely, majority voting eases the path for change but also for reversal. In a highly politically polarized environment, if control of Congress passes back and forth between two parties, the end of the filibuster in the Senate could enhance legal uncertainty by further enabling revenge governance.

Second, increased political polarization makes it much more difficult for the nation to address and reach compromise on a series of important substantive issues, such as counteracting climate change or better adapting to it; scaling back increasing federal budget deficits; and repairing, replacing, and updating the nation's aging infrastructure, to name just a few concerns. The longer decisions are delayed on these and other important questions the more difficult it will be to tackle them as damage accumulates in the meantime.

Third, political polarization erodes not only trust in government—how can you trust government when it is in the "hands of the other side"?—but also in each other. Party allegiance has become tribal in nature, fracturing families and friendships and eroding the social glue that keeps societies together.[21] If the United States were not so geographically integrated, I suspect there would be substantial support for splitting the country between its red and blue citizens if it could somehow be done (it can't). Author William Bishop has documented in his widely read *The Big Sort* that people are doing the next closest thing: sorting themselves into neighborhoods and workplaces composed of those who share roughly the same political views. Sorting reduces the frequency of interactions with people from other backgrounds, races, religions, and political views, reducing understanding and empathy for others, contributing to or at least preventing the healing of the rifts that are dividing this country.

With adults in this country already so divided politically, with more voters viewing public policy issues and even facts through a political lens, it is tempting to give up hope. Indeed, Kahneman himself is skeptical, if not pessimistic, that voters' tendencies to be governed by system 1 thinking can be fundamentally altered, pointing to statistical evidence suggesting that roughly 70 percent of voting results can be explained by voters' initial reaction to pictures of people, which is a system 1 response.[22] In a similar vein, Haidt makes a compelling claim that the basic ingredients that determine our political stances in life or those mental "frameworks" referred to earlier—caring, fairness, loyalty, sanctity—are genetic, and that liberals and conservatives have different mixes of these traits. If we are hard-wired at birth to be either blue or red when we become adults, then is there any basis for believing that our current politically based divisions will narrow in the future?

In the balance of this chapter, I hope to convince you that the answer to this question is yes. Even the claim that political stances have a genetic basis, at least in part, does not mean that political beliefs are immutable, or at the very least, that we must be incapable, as many of us seem to be right now, of treating those with very different political views with respect. We may be born with genetic predispositions that favor one political stance over another, but actual life experience determines which path we will follow, and it needn't be a straight one. People can and do change their minds. Haidt himself invokes neuroscientist Gary Marcus' definition of "innateness," which essentially explains Haidt's own thesis: "Nature provides a first draft, which experience then revises. . . . 'Built-in' does not mean unmalleable; it means *organized in advance of experience*"[23] (emphasis in original).

Much of our "experience" comes from our parents, friends, and coworkers, and their political attitudes or tendencies clearly affect ours. But teachers, too, can and do play a critical role in shaping how and what you think, not only through the content they deliver but how they do it. Richard Nisbett, a psychologist at the University of Michigan who has sparred with Kahneman and Tversky, has conducted experiments showing how people can change their minds once they are given new information and explanations that might cause them to do so. [24] This is especially true of juries, which are more likely to come to different conclusions after they hear both sides of a case rather than just one.[25]

Indeed, another way to define the fundamental purpose of education is to view it as the way society—at least our democratic society—has chosen to equip students with the skills and, ideally, the inclination, to use system 2 thinking more frequently, not just as students but when they become adults. Education shapes young adults much as sculptors shape clay before it is fired in a kiln to become pottery. Human beings and society, however, function best when even adults have some "putty" in them so they can adapt their views and skills to changed circumstances. Once we are fired clay, we are stuck in our ways and can't adapt. That is a dangerous way to live when the world is constantly changing. Thus, another function of education is to give us all a putty mindset so that, as individuals acting alone and collectively, we can adapt to change.

For example, when your system 2 is working properly, you are also open-minded, or open to persuasion by the facts that certain courses of action are better than others. While education gives us mental frameworks for considering or processing these facts—as an economist, for example, I have been taught to weigh costs and benefits and to have a theory of how economies behave—system 2 rational thought allows for the possibility that our initial impulses might be wrong. As Mahatma Gandhi once put it: "It is unwise to be too sure of one's own wisdom. It is healthy to be reminded that the strongest might weaken and the wisest might err."[26]

Intellectual modesty and curiosity are difficult to maintain at any time, but especially in these times when it has become all too easy to react out of fear, perhaps the strongest trigger of system 1 behavior, which closes minds and reinforces our tribal tendencies. In recent times, there has been much to be fearful about. *New York Times* columnist David Brooks observes that we live in "an era defined by fear,"[27] citing fear from continued acts of foreign and domestic terrorism as well as the fear so many Americans have about their future and that of their children. Unfortunately, too many of our political leaders have found that the best way to ensure they remain in or get those leadership jobs is to play to those fears.

In a cover story for *The Atlantic* in early 2019, Charles Duhigg quotes Harvard's Steve Jarding making precisely this point: "The essence of [political] campaigns today is anger and fear. That's how you win."[28] Duhigg shows how dressing up arguments in claims of morality and directing anger toward opponents is a powerful strategy for gaining and remaining in political office.

But anger and fear can also too easily lead to a vicious cycle, with the "losers" in one round plotting revenge in the next round. It is already apparent how this vicious cycle has played out in American politics over the past two decades. Vicious cycles of revenge in other times and places have resulted in far more catastrophic results. The vengeful reaction of the citizens and leaders of the allied victors of World War I in forcing Germany to submit to draconian reparations that were criticized at the time by British economist John Maynard Keynes in his *Economic Consequences of Peace,* played a large role, as did the Depression, in Hitler's rise and the horrors of World War II.

My Brookings colleague Darrell West has written eloquently and sensibly about how the United States, through various measures, can begin to repair the deep divisions in our country that threaten our democracy in his thoughtful book *Divided Politics Divided Nation.*[29] Rather than outline another set of suggestions, I focus here on a single idea: instructing students in a wide variety of classroom settings and subjects through debate techniques that require oral advocacy, based on fact-based research and reason, of both sides (or possibly more) of various issues. I do not claim this is the only answer, or the best answer, to the partisan rancor that plagues us. But over time—presuming we have it—I believe DCI would materially help bridge some of our social and political divisions, and that should be enough to recommend it. DCI also has the advantage of building on and strengthening an institution—public K–12 education—whose health a vast majority of Americans believe is essential to our having a positive economic and political future.

Civic Benefits of Debate-Centered Instruction

The main argument for DCI in high school, and possibly in middle school or earlier, as outlined in the last chapter, is not only to improve education for students while they are in school but to show them the fun and the benefits of continuing to learn throughout their lives. A strong incidental result of giving young people the experience of debating two or more sides of many topics is that it increases the odds that when they become adults they will be more likely to appreciate the complexities in most issues that affect the collective well-being of their communities and country. In the best of worlds—which is possible; don't give up—debate training that compels students to research and argue at least two sides of multiple issues should make more people coming out of school less susceptible to falling into the trap of living in and obtaining information from a preference or filter bubble, on social media, television, print media, or in real human interactions (yes, those still exist, too, even in this age of personal computers and smart-phones). Students, and later, when they become adults, are less likely, for example, to view proponents taking the "other side" of any given issue as "the enemy" when they have frequently had to vigorously argue on behalf of "other sides." Indeed, given the rapidly growing power of social media to create and reinforce preference bubbles, the deploy-ment of DCI in classrooms cannot happen soon enough.

As the fictional character Atticus Finch in *To Kill a Mockingbird* fa-mously stated: "You never really understand a person until you con-sider things from his point of view, until you climb inside of his skin and walk around in it."[30] This is precisely what active participation in debate promotes: understanding other points of view, which in the pro-cess induces people to more frequently use their system 2 thinking in Kahneman's terminology, or to act more like riders than elephants in Haidt's.

Sarah Ryan of Baruch College proposed in 2006 incorporating debate for essentially these reasons even at the college level, in an in-troductory civics course,[31] although by the time students reach college their mental structures are likely to be more hardened than they are at younger ages, which is the reason my focus here has been mainly at the high school and earlier grades. This is especially so in this age of social media when our political identities get locked in and become harder to change without loss of face and friends. Middle and high school stu-dents are less likely than older students and adults to have fully formed political views, let alone express them online (with the possible excep-tion of gun control in the wake of the student-led organized activity in the wake of the 2017 mass shooting at Marjorie Stoneman High School in Parkland, Florida). If students are taught to be more open-minded when they are younger, they may bring that mindset to their future social media activity—assuming it will exist in anything like its cur-rent form several years, let alone one or two decades, from now.

Every single one of the former competitive debaters I spoke with in researching this book echoed these sentiments. Certainly, this may be something of a self-selected sample, and competitive debate is not the same as the DCI I am recommending for classroom teaching. But DCI should have at least somewhat similar positive effects because it teaches students the same skills. The positive effects should also grow as the number of classes in which it is used increases—analogous to the positive relationship doctors observe between doses of medicine and responses, up to a point when the effects flatten out.

Cynics will say it is delusional to think anything can change the fact that most voting is driven more by emotion than reason. But that pessimism is premised on voting populations having little or no direct training in understanding, let alone having to advocate orally, opposite sides of positions on many topics. In other words, predictions about the behavior of the voting public that presuppose new voters will continue to be educated in the same way as in the past—without the benefits of acquiring debate skills—assume a result without taking account of how changes in educational instruction should change how future voters make decisions, in both their private lives and in how they vote.

What about citizens' exposure to the now seemingly endless presidential debates and candidate debates for lesser offices? Does this provide a close substitute for what I am advocating? The short answer is no. Watching something on TV is entirely different than doing it, whether it is playing a sport or having to orally defend a position on any given issue, let alone having to research and advocate different sides of that issue. The process of doing the latter, across several years of schooling and multiple topics, would instill and develop skills that a vast majority of voters simply do not have today in the United States, or any other democracy for that matter.

Moreover, candidate debates for political office, especially presidential debates,[32] bear little resemblance to either competitive debates in school or to the structured classroom debates I have proposed students participate in as a matter of routine. Although both political and school debates have time limits for the main presentations, answers to questions, and periods for response, the limits are much shorter for candidate debates—allowing enough time for sound bites and not much more. In the political arena, the perceived character and past behavior, public and private, of the participants matters for audience members, who, in effect, act as employers hiring job candidates. In school debates, however, participants are judged on the substance of their arguments, not on who they are (although judges in competitive debate tournaments, especially after the preliminary rounds are over, often can't help but take some account of a team's reputation, just as teachers and peers in the classroom are somewhat influenced by the reputation of the debating students).

Likewise, style can easily trump (no pun intended) substance in a political setting, much more than in the classroom. Two clear examples of this come to mind: when Ronald Reagan famously one-lined then President Carter in the 1980 presidential debates by simply saying "There you go again" and when vice presidential candidate and then Senator Lloyd Bentsen's putdown of his counterpart, then Senator Dan Quayle, "Senator, I served with Jack Kennedy. I knew Jack Kennedy. Jack Kennedy was a friend of mine. Senator, you're no Jack Kennedy." Even these barbs do not change the fact that, until the age of Trump, presidential debates were generally civil in nature, in this sense similar to school debates.

In his 2016 presidential run and since taking office, President Trump has changed the rules. Name calling, insults, and repeated statements having little or no factual basis—all expressly out of bounds in school debates—are central features of Trump's debating style and of his direct communication with the public. Only time will tell whether "anything goes" has become acceptable in future political contests, especially at the presidential level, or whether there is something unique to President Trump that allows him, and only him, to get away with breaking conventional debate and civic norms.

Finally, candidate statements are "fact-checked" by the news media, which is done after any false or misleading claims are made—when much of the public may not be paying attention—and also in a climate when much of the media is not trusted or where voter trust exists only for certain sources of information (such as the high confidence Republicans place in Fox News and Democrats in MSNBC and CNN, for example). False statements made by debate teams in tournaments can lead to their elimination, while individuals misstating facts in front of their teachers almost surely will be penalized in some fashion.

Before jumping to the conclusion that these differences between political and classroom debates are inevitable, keep in mind how the mindset of the audience influences how debates are conducted. In competitive debate tournaments in high school and college, for example, debaters say they size up the judge before they begin talking. If the judge is a lay person, a parent, or a friend of a parent, as is common in the early rounds of high school debate tournaments, debaters will slow their rate of speech and give more importance to persuasion than to quickly spitting out arguments and refuting them so they win the "flow," or the standard debate scorecard that debate-trained judges commonly use. Debaters also will say that lay judges are more likely to reward style over substance, certainly when compared to debate-trained judges. Likewise, in the classroom, students instructed in debate techniques may speak differently when practicing in front of their peers than when debating in front of an entire classroom and judged by a teacher.

Political candidates are no different. Few if any members of their audiences—in person or on television since candidate debates were first broadcast in 1960—have had formal debate training or been schooled in researching and orally advocating both sides of multiple propositions. So far, the audience for these debates, the voting electorate, is akin to the lay judge at school debate tournaments who tends to give more points to debaters with clever zingers than to those that may present more or better evidence or whose arguments are more logical. Most of those in "political audiences" also already have their minds made up and watch the debates to reinforce or validate their prior beliefs, to be entertained, or some combination of the two.

Now imagine candidate debates in front of audiences composed of substantial numbers of voters who have had formal debate training, whether those voters lean in one direction or another before debates begin. For debate-trained listeners, one-liners like "There you go again" are much more likely to fall on deaf ears. Because they have had to do it themselves, listeners who have actively debated will be much more likely to listen closely to the facts and logic the candidates present than to their glibness or their style. And speaking of facts, students well versed in debating are likelier to give more credit to candidates who tell the truth, since they were judged that way in their own classes growing up. Similarly, voters with school debate experience are less likely to be persuaded by fear mongering and the attack ads routinely seen on television or social media during political campaigns, since appeals of this kind would not have been tolerated in their school debates. For all these reasons, as the share of the voting electorate with debate training increases, there is at least some reason to believe that political candidate debates and campaigns would become more substantive and less negative.

Each of the foregoing claims are testable hypotheses, and as more schools implement DCI, more data will exist for researchers to determine whether these claims hold up. My own debating experience, coupled with interviews of many ex-debaters and debate coaches in the course of researching this book, supports what lawyers would call a *prima facie* case, or a rebuttable presumption, that debate training helps those who have had it maintain a more open mind on a wide range of political issues than otherwise would be the case.

This isn't to say that voters are blank slates, like juries are supposed to be (but never completely are). They come into debates, or watch television or social media ads, with political predispositions, still very much affected by the party affiliations of the parents, peers, and coworkers, though not necessarily in that order.

Voters, even those trained in debate, also inevitably will have certain biases—the same kind of biases in reasoning that Nobel prize winning scholars like Daniel Kahneman and Richard Thaler, and a host of other behavioral economists and psychologists these two have inspired, have identified over the years. For example, of clear relevance in a political context, behavioral social scientists have shown that people often exhibit "confirmation bias," the tendency to seek out only that information that confirms preexisting views. Social media and cable TV both enable people to live in a political echo chamber where they hear or read only what they want to hear or read. Another common bias that researchers have identified is something economists call "hyperbolic discounting," which means people giving too little weight to the long-run impacts of their decisions. This is one of the reasons Congress has so far not meaningfully reined in long-run federal deficits or tackled climate change. In case you're wondering how many other types of bias can and do affect people's decisions, one author reports that *Wikipedia* counts at least 185 of them.[33]

DCI training is not going to remove the predispositions or biases of students. I simply claim that people's minds are likely to become more malleable—susceptible to reason and evidence—the more debate training individuals acquire. Similarly, debate training should make students, before they become adults, more aware of biases or potential sources of bias, by instilling a mindset of critical thinking.

I also do not claim that every student must acquire debate skills for our politics to change when they become adults. If only a small percent of the voting population gains these skills, that could make the difference in many elections, and more difference over time as more schools implement debate techniques in the classroom and students develop the open mindset that debating cultivates.

Implications of the Rebuttable Presumption that DCI Should Improve Our Politics

Several propositions, testable in theory and logical in fact, follow from the foregoing observations. First, as more voters engage system 2 thinking when they vote, party attachment, though not necessarily party affiliation, should weaken. Accordingly, voters should be less likely to agree with the consensus positions of their parties on all issues, and may, over time, vote straight party tickets less frequently. I would not expect this effect to be as strong, or perhaps even evident, however, in elections for lesser offices, at the state and local levels, where ideological differences are not likely to be as intensely held as on national issues and where the outcomes depend heavily on both name recognition and party identity of the candidates.

There is some dispute among political analysts about the extent to which voters already have been moving away from political parties. Stanford political scientist Morris Fiorina points to survey evidence showing the share of the electorate identifying as "independent" has risen over time, to the point where independents now constitute a plurality of all voters.[34] As an incidental matter, Fiorina argues that this evidence belies claims that the majority of the electorate are becoming more politically polarized. But political analyst Ruy Teixeira counters that most independents "lean" toward one of the two parties, so the true number of political independents is vastly overstated by surveys reporting party affiliation or independent status.[35] Teixeira's perspective, if true, would be consistent with claims of growing polarization among voters. It isn't necessary to determine which of these two positions is mostly right or wrong; whatever the underlying trends in the electorate, the larger the share of voters who have had debate training as students, the weaker the party attachments are likely to be in the voting public over time.

Second, increasing debate education eventually should lead to more diversity of thought within parties and less tendency to "outsource" one's thinking about political issues to party leaders. Admittedly, there have always been different wings in each of the parties that represent different combinations of views on a host of domestic and foreign policy issues, but those differences have been eroding over time, more among Republicans, it seems, than Democrats. As a result, both parties are becoming more ideologically homogeneous.

I am old enough, for example, to remember the sharp divisions between more establishment Republicans, including "liberal" Republicans like former New York Governor and Vice President Nelson Rockefeller, and conservatives, predominantly from Southern and Western states. This philosophical split has narrowed over time, however, with conservatives winning the battle for the soul of the Republican party, although the rise of Donald Trump has redefined what it means to be a conservative. Many "Never Trumpers" adhere to classic conservative positions—on free trade, fiscal prudence, and openness toward immigrants (and a pathway to citizenship for immigrants who came here unlawfully)—which Donald Trump has abandoned in a full-throated way, persuading the vast majority of those who now call themselves Republicans to agree with him. Meanwhile, "liberal Republicans" (some call them RINOs, or Republicans in Name Only) have essentially disappeared.

The modern, post-civil rights Democratic party also, historically, has been divided, perhaps more deeply than Republicans, between its two dominant wings: moderates and liberals or "progressives." During my late teens, this division manifested itself most sharply over foreign policy, specifically U.S. engagement in the Vietnam War. In more recent decades, Democrats have split more on domestic policy issues. For example, during the 2020 presidential campaign, virtually all of the candidates endorsed the goals of ensuring that all Americans have health insurance and of dramatically reducing carbon dioxide emissions. The differences, although significant, were largely over timing and details on how to realize these goals.

An electorate composed of an increasing share of voters having had debate training in their student years presumably would not be as ideologically homogeneous as both parties seem to be becoming. Armed with the research and advocacy skills developed through debate training, adults should be more likely to take pragmatic positions issue-by-issue. If this occurred, there would be more diversity of views within each party. If that happened, there would be less partisanship, which would make governing easier.

Third, if voters become less firmly attached to or affiliated with political parties, this could facilitate the growth of a third, or possibly other, parties organized perhaps around one or two single issues, which may or may not be permanent. From a purely electoral perspective, this is not unambiguously a good thing; it depends on where one sits. Even without winning elections, the presence of a third-party candidate in a very close presidential election could tip the election in favor of the candidate from one of the two main parties, as many believe Ralph Nader did in 2000, by tilting the outcome to George W. Bush, and again in 2016, when votes for Jill Stein arguably helped Donald Trump win the presidency (although votes for libertarian Gary Johnson may have come at the expense of Trump's). Even in a not-as-close election, in 1993, the much more popular candidacy of Ross Perot is believed by many to have cost George H. W. Bush a second term.

A stronger and less ambiguous argument for more frequent third-party presidential runs, which could be the outcome of a more debate-educated citizenry, is that alternative candidates who attract a sizeable vote count could push the policy of the winning candidate, or succeeding ones, in a favorable direction. This has happened in the past and could occur more frequently in the future. Take, for example, Theodore Roosevelt's Bull Moose third-party challenge in 1912, which many historians credit for swinging that election to Woodrow Wilson and away from Roosevelt's Republican challenger, William Howard Taft. Roosevelt's progressive reform agenda—calling for women's suffrage, a minimum wage, and insurance for seniors—was ahead of its time but, eventually, was adopted as national policy. Likewise, Ross Perot mounted a strong third-party challenge in the 1992 presidential race, and though he lost, the strong electoral support for his deficit-reduction message influenced the winner, Bill Clinton, to give deficit reduction high priority twice in his two terms, first in 1993 and again in 1997.

There are at least two reasons, however, why an electorate populated with more debate-trained voters might reduce the frequency and/or potency of third-party challenges. One reason is that if the two main parties become more philosophically or ideologically diverse, as predicted, there would be less pressure and support for independent candidacies advocating issues that the "bigger tent" parties would then accommodate.

A second reason is that, a more debate-trained electorate may be more likely to embrace pragmatic, less ideological and more moderate positions on a wide range of public policy issues—and thus tend to support candidates who embrace a similar approach—affording fewer opportunities for moderate third-party candidates to emerge. Admittedly, not every debater is a political moderate. To the contrary, there are notable elected officials in public life whose views are far from centrist, and debate experience may, indeed, have helped them defend those positions. But my informal polling of former debaters confirms my own experience: once you are not only exposed to contrary views but must research and orally defend them, you inevitably see that most issues are not black-and-white but a shade of gray. That mindset should lend greater support within both parties in primary elections for moderate candidates, counteracting current tendencies toward more extreme positions at the primary stage.

A Debate-Educated Citizenry Is Healthy for Democracy

It may sound utopian to some readers to claim that a single instructional technique implemented in high school or middle school, if not earlier, has the potential for improving our democracy, but that may be only because most readers have not had formal debate training in school. Its power cannot be overstated. Debate training would fundamentally improve the way students think about virtually everything in their lives. It would engage their interest in learning, but more important, it would elevate the role of system 2 thinking in their lives—reason over emotion.

Not all students would gain the same benefits, and, thus, not all students—when they become adults—would apply the critical thinking skills they develop in school as a result of DCI to all their decisions. But it would satisfy historian Jon Meacham's plea that America "give reason a chance."[36]

More people applying reason more often in their lives cannot help but be a plus for democracy. An effective democracy presupposes that enough citizens demand of their elected representatives that they have enough of an open mind to make those decisions that affect everyone's lives based on fact and evidence, not on ideological rigidity. When elected leaders operate in this way, they are also open to the kinds of compromises that allow government to function well.

Americans now have little confidence that their federal government and their leaders act this way at all. And they are right to feel this way. The polarized divisions in our country have led to this outcome.

It is hard to keep count of all the articles and books that offer analyses and, less frequently, solutions for polarization and its pernicious consequences for democracy and for our society. Nonetheless, various "political process" experiments have been tried in recent years in the United States and elsewhere to address the problem.[37] One approach with positive results in multiple countries is "guided deliberation," in which controversial issues are delegated to small but representative groups of citizens to hash out solutions, which are then voted on by legislatures or even entire voting populations, such as referendums. Ireland used such a "Citizen's Assembly" to address abortion, while France has used a variation of the idea to address inequality issues raised by the Yellow Vest movement. In the United States, San Francisco, Minneapolis, and Maine have used "rank choice" voting, in which voters do not simply vote for a single candidate but rank them in order of preference—a mechanism that helps ensure that the winners are the ones most broadly acceptable to the electorate.[38] California has used public hearings before initiatives are put to statewide referenda as a way of educating the public about the issues at stake.

These are all potentially good ideas, and further experimentation with them should be encouraged. They have two things in common. One is that each process would benefit if the participants had formal debate training earlier in life, so that they bring with them to these tasks the knowledge that all issues have at least two sides, and are capable of assessing the arguments and those who advance them with respect rather than reflexive rejection or even hate.

Second, each of these alternative ideas very likely sounded utopian in the beginning, yet each is making headway in the real world. Think of DCI the same way: perhaps utopian to some today but conventional wisdom at some point tomorrow.

Finally, it is possible to take lessons from debate and apply them in the adult world right away, not necessarily to change minds but at least to promote civility and respect and begin to bridge the divide that separates too many of us in our politically polarized world. Better Angels is a young, but growing organization dedicated to this principle—that simply getting people with sharply different political mindsets into the same room talking with each other in a civil way, using a debate style format, reduces the anger and distrust among those on each side of the red-blue divide. It seems to be working.[39] Hopefully, it will scale. Eventually, in a world in which all adults have debate training in formal schooling, it wouldn't be necessary.

FIVE

Debating Skills Are Not Just for Future Lawyers

The perception is widespread that debate is good only for training law-yers. Cy Smith, a successful Baltimore trial lawyer, summed it up when he realized that, in preparing for one of his many trials, as he was laying out his proof for an upcoming trial, he was essentially doing the same thing he had done as a competitive debater in both high school and in four years at Dartmouth (where, after graduation, he served as an as-sistant debate coach before going to law school). I have heard similar stories from other former competitive debaters who became lawyers. Not surprisingly, many politicians are both former lawyers and former competitive debaters, which explains why, with a few exceptions, I ex-cluded from the appendix to the first chapter most current or former elected officials. Had I not done so, the list would have been too long!

For a similar reason, I will not spend time in this chapter recounting the many ways that debate, whether competitive or in the classroom, helps train future lawyers, especially litigators at the trial and appellate levels. I will make only two points about debate and law before moving on. Although most litigators specialize in representing only one side of disputes—either plaintiffs or defendants—good attorneys must always anticipate and, thus, put themselves in the shoes of the other side. Likewise, even transactional lawyers—those who prepare all kinds of legal documents: contracts, wills, divorce agreements, and like—also must anticipate potential disputes and try to resolve them up front. Competitive debate helps prepare attorneys to do all these things.

But debate, whether engaged in competitively or through classroom instruction, is not just for lawyers and the few who make it to the bench as judges. I hope to convince you in this chapter that debating and evidence-based argumentation skills are useful, and in many cases essential, for employers; entrepreneurs and employees, including teachers (many of them speech and debate teachers and coaches); and those who work in a wide variety of other jobs and careers, blue and white collar.

The workplace benefits of debate could not be more important at this time in our nation's—and even the world's—history, when there is so much angst about the potential threat to jobs and wages generated by continuing advances in software, artificial intelligence, and robotics. I will not claim that having debate skills will protect you from these and other technological advances and their inevitable ripple effects through the workforce and the economy. Rather, I will argue that having such skills is one important way you, your children, and society will be better prepared to adapt to continuing advances in technology of whatever form.

Debate Experience Helps Entrepreneurs

I spent nearly a decade of my life, from 2003 to 2012, as a vice president and research director at the Kauffman Foundation, the nation's leading foundation financing research relating to entrepreneurship as well as various programs aimed at facilitating the emergence and growth of "entrepreneurship eco-systems," or communities where entrepreneurs and those who assist them (accountants, lawyers, and financiers, among others) frequently interact and help each other. While I was there, and since I moved on, the foundation has also helped build a community of scholars who have produced a growing mountain of findings about entrepreneurs and their importance to any economy. Together with colleagues I met there and since, I have been able in a small way to contribute to that effort.[1] In a nutshell, the following is all you need to know, at least for purposes of this book, about what this research has found:

- Entrepreneurs, who start and build businesses by choice rather than by necessity, are critical for developing and commercializing innovations, which are the most important sources of economic growth and, thus, growth in standards of living in the long run.

- There has been a precipitous drop in annual new firm formation in the United States following the 2008 financial crisis, from around 600,000 to roughly 400,000.[2] A variety of explanations have been advanced for this decline, with no apparent consensus on the most important reasons. I don't know of any expert who doubts that a return to the new firm formation levels pre-2008 would be a good thing, as would any developments that increase the odds of survival for new firms or the growth rates of those that do survive.

Debate training can help those who choose an entrepreneurial path because debate skills are ideal for addressing the multiple audiences that successful entrepreneurs must reach. Entrepreneurs launching their business often, at some point, seek outside funding—whether from friends and family, angel investors, or, in much rarer cases, venture capitalists. To do this successfully, company founders must prepare and hone their "pitch," typically a PowerPoint presentation no longer than ten pages that is also an outline for a prepared talk aimed at persuading others to invest in the enterprise. The investor pitch is analogous to the first affirmative speech in a formal debate.

The debate analogy doesn't stop there. Entrepreneurs seeking funding must also prepare thoroughly to answer tough questions about their business plan, product, and "exit strategy"—that is, whether they are seeking to grow the company and perhaps take it public one day or expect to expand the business to the point where it can be profitably sold at a large "multiple" (sales price divided by the total amounts invested) to another company. The process of anticipating and preparing responses to a wide range of conceivable questions, doubts, and objections in a way to convert any skepticism to enthusiasm is very much what a formal debater does in his or her first or second affirmative rebuttal or, in a less formal classroom setting, what a student must do to respond to any challenges to his or her initial argument or claim.

Entrepreneurs must make variations of the investor pitch to potential employees, especially initial hires, who may be paid much as an investor would be, through the grant of stock or stock options. Likewise, suppliers to and customers of early stage companies often invest in them as well. One expert on entrepreneurship, Amar Bhide of Tufts University, has written an entire book on how customers of start-ups are analogous to the venture capitalists who fund them.[3] All of these parties must be persuaded, in one fashion or another, to take some risk to do business with entrepreneurs. The art of persuasion is perhaps best honed through debate, where the main objective is to convince an audience to agree with the presenter. What better training for entrepreneurship than debate can there be?

Employers Should Value Debate Skills

Start-ups are just a small fraction of the employers in the U.S. economy and, for that matter, in all developed country economies. Most businesses have been around a while, surely longer than the first few years of any start-up's life. Indeed, one possible reason for the sluggish growth of productivity in the United States in recent decades is that the business structure is aging—that is, surviving businesses are getting older.[4] Older firms, like older people, can be less likely to innovate or welcome innovation, something that is key to economic progress and rising living standards.

New products, services, or methods of production typically require many more people than a single genius with a sudden solution to a tough problem. Sure, having that genius as a spark is important, but not all great ideas, even those successfully patented or deserving of a Nobel prize, are what consumers or other businesses will want to buy. To be commercially successful, new ideas must be embodied in just the right kind of product as well as designed, manufactured, marketed, and distributed in the right way and with the right timing. Plenty of great ideas fail in the marketplace because they either cannot be produced or delivered at a price point that will attract purchasers, they haven't been sold in a way that captures the public's imagination, or the timing was a bit off. Think of the Edsel in the automotive industry, the NEXT computer invented by Steve Jobs, and many other seemingly can't-miss innovations that flopped because the market for one reason or another wasn't ready for them.

There are countless theories and management books about how firms can best be structured and managed to promote innovation. My takeaway from this vast literature is that the best commercial successes are achieved with innovation "teams," whose members have many kinds of experiences, both within the firm and before arriving there. In addition, innovation in larger companies often is walled off or insulated from the rest of the firm's bureaucracy in a "skunkworks" type setting (a building or set of offices separated from the rest of the company) so the participants are freer to think outside the box and then come back to managers who are open-minded enough to see the opportunities innovations open up. Even then, the firm's leaders must decide on a roll-out strategy: to go "big" right away or to test the idea with a small group of the firm's customers, and then to proceed gradually. Either way, innovations are only as successful as their implementation. Famed venture capitalist John Doerr probably understated the importance of new ideas when he proclaimed that "ideas are easy. It's execution that's everything." But his next sentence was certainly on the money: *"And it takes a team to win"*[5] (emphasis added).

Innovation and its execution depend on a workplace environment that fosters creativity, where workers and supervisors don't say no to ideas off the bat but also constantly challenge proponents of new ideas to address potential objections in a way that doesn't personally threaten them. In other words, in a culture that separates the ideas from those who are presenting or challenging them.

This description reads a lot like a school debate. And that is precisely why employers that foster the *right kind* of debate-like cultures are also well positioned to promote innovation, which is key to any firm's survival and growth.

By "right kind," I mean a culture that encourages all employees to make their views known and to develop skills to defend their positions, whether in the form of suggestions for improvements, ideas for new products or services, or complaints. Of course, employees won't speak up unless they know they will not be punished and, ideally, will be rewarded in some fashion by their supervisors or upper level managers. This means that debate cultures are set from the top so that good ideas can percolate from the bottom up. Just as important, workers must not be penalized for proposing ideas that, after thorough vetting— arguments and counterarguments—are ultimately rejected. People with debate experience have the training to engage in this kind of give and take, but a work culture that encourages it can be established and maintained only if supervisors and managers themselves have debate training or think like debaters.

The right kind of work culture also matches the culture of competitive or classroom debate in school: one that allows civil discourse, without name calling, that separates arguments from those making them. As one of the nation's leading rhetorical scholars, David Zarefksy of Northwestern University, has written, true debates are successful when "people respect each other regardless of the beliefs they espouse. Disagreements take place over standpoints, not individuals."[6]

There is a big difference between vigorous argument and screaming matches. People can walk away from the former respecting those who disagree with them. In screaming matches, people walk away angry at each other. Angry people are more likely to hold grudges against people who disagree with them. Anger and grudges are not conducive to the cooperation necessary to make any organization—for profit or nonprofit—work effectively.

I have worked in many different organizations in my life, over nearly five decades, in the private and nonprofit sector and in government, and can attest to the positive experience that healthy debates can foster—though few of my colleagues have had the debate training I recommend here (or maybe more had training and I didn't know). I can also attest to the demoralizing impact the wrong kind of work culture can have on any organization, its current productivity, and on developing (or not developing) innovations to help workers and consumers.

Perhaps the best-known example of a company literally built explicitly around a debate-centered work environment is the highly successful hedge fund Bridgewater, founded by Ray Dalio, who has written a book, *Principles*, that explains the human side of his company's success. Dalio uses two terms throughout the book to describe the way he ran Bridgewater and what the company demands of its employees: "radical transparency" and "open-mindedness." To be sure, Bridgewater owes much of its success to an increasingly sophisticated financial asset prediction model and data analytics platform that has been able to sniff out and capitalize on asset mispricings for the benefit of the firm's investors and managers. But Dalio makes clear that Bridgewater was able to develop and refine its technology—which is also supplemented by human judgment—through a constant process of debate among his employees and partners. Indeed, one gets the impression from reading his book that Bridgewater is one big financial debate society, where all employees must constantly be transparent in what they are claiming and open-minded to the ideas of others.

Dalio also makes clear that debate is instrumental in the way his firm hires new employees and is used to help screen out new hires who do not appear to fit into Bridgewater's unique culture: "One way you can tell how well a talented rookie will do relative to a proven star is to get them into a debate with each other and see how well they each hold up."[7] Admittedly, not every job at every firm requires a test that many may view as more suitable for professional athletes, where this kind of direct competition is common. Nonetheless, Dalio's advice applies to many white- and blue-collar jobs, especially at meritocratic companies that prize and reward excellence. What better way to prepare for such work environments than to have many mini-debate experiences as early as middle school, if not later in high school as well?

To be clear, Dalio makes no bones about how difficult it is to work for Bridgewater. He insists on hiring and retaining only the best and letting people who don't fit in go elsewhere—though not without first giving them a chance to work in other parts of his company if they are not doing well in their current positions. It is hard to argue with Bridgewater's success. Since its founding in 1975, assets under management have grown from essentially zero to over $160 billion.[8]

The importance of healthy internal debate is implicit in many other companies and industries where firms are built on teamwork for both innovation and implementation. That is because teams cannot be successful unless their members have enough respect for each other to be able to take the risks of engaging in constructive debates with the objective of reaching an end result that moves the organization, or its subunits, in a positive direction—toward greater profitability, whether by increased sales, reduced expenses, or some combination of the two.

Teamwork at the CEO level, among his or her direct reports, and with lower level employees is especially important for innovating. Hal Gregersen, executive director of the MIT Leadership Center, explains that good leaders of any organization do not assume they have all the answers but, instead, use questions to encourage "fresh thinking." Questions that reach for out of-the-box solutions are especially important for stimulating innovation. Gregersen recounts "hearing from executives at one company that the boss always surprised his top team by being willing to hear out even the craziest ideas." He suggests that, in brainstorming, "go for high volume and do not edit [ideas] in progress."[9] That is the best way, he explains, for teams to break a seemingly insurmountable impasse.

Brainstorming is unlikely to be successful, however, unless everyone in the room feels comfortable with honest debate, conversations that separate the ideas from the persons suggesting them. That is precisely the kind of classroom environment found in the Boston and Chicago schools that are implementing debate or argument-centered instruction, where no idea or comment is swatted away, along with the dignity of the person advancing it. Instead, teachers make sure to compliment students for taking the risk to speak up and then challenge the rest of the class by asking "Can anyone think of a better answer or explanation?" Where company leaders have fostered the same kind of culture within their organizations, they maximize chances for successful innovation.

Several now iconic California-based young companies are leading exemplars of how a team-oriented business culture, led from the top, can drive a company's success. Management consultant Robert Bruce Shaw demonstrates this in his 2019 book *Extreme Teams*, which documents how teamwork has been essential to the rise of Pixar, Netflix, and Airbnb, among other "cutting-edge" companies.[10] Teamwork doesn't mean total harmony all the time. Teams are successful when all members are focused on achieving a common objective and are able to tolerate, and indeed thrive, on conflict. Shaw says that "extreme teams"—the kind he extolls in his book—"are biased in favor of conflict, even encouraging it among their members. These teams believe that fighting over the right issues results in better outcomes."[11] This kind of productive conflict can exist, however, only so long as team members are able to separate arguments from personalities. Otherwise, arguments can lead to personal frictions and, over time, destroy the glue or the culture that enables teams to be successful. One of the core skills debate training teaches is to take the personality out of the argumentation, yet another reason why DCI is ideal for both students' future workplace success and for the companies or institutions that employ them (or which they launch themselves!).

Having a team-oriented company culture has been recognized in two of the most successful tech giants. In their original incarnations, both Microsoft and Apple were run as founder-led autocracies, as are many successful non-tech companies. Both Bill Gates, in the case of Microsoft, and Steve Jobs, at Apple, reportedly interrogated employees in highly argumentative fashions, mixing attacks on ideas with which they disagreed with personal attacks on those who offered them. Even Bill Gates' wife Melinda, who once worked at Microsoft and had major managerial responsibilities, has described Microsoft's work environment as being "so brash, so argumentative and competitive," that she often felt she didn't "belong."[12] It apparently was not much different at Apple.[13]

I cannot overstate how much this kind of workplace environment is not what I have in mind in suggesting that firms adopt or develop a debate-centric work culture. There was technically "debate" and "argument" in the founder-led stages of Microsoft's and Apple's lives, but it was conducted in a personal, take-no-prisoners' way that could have backfired had it not been for the creative genius of each founder. An autocratic management style and work environment, however, will not carry any company once the founder has voluntarily left or downgraded his own role (in the case of Gates) or passed away (in the case of Jobs). At that point, if the company is not headed by leaders devoted to building loyalty of employees by valuing their input and by promoting healthy debates among them, then it will stagnate at best, or decline, or worse.

Both tech giants have since surpassed the successes created by their founders by moving away from founder autocracy. For example, while Microsoft's post-Gates success under Satya Nadella has been largely attributed to his decision to focus the company around the "cloud" and the process of breaking up the Windows unit,[14] Nadella has also changed Microsoft's culture, putting much more emphasis on teamwork than cutthroat competition among the firm's employees.[15] One has a sense, from the outside at least, that Microsoft's engineers, marketers, and financiers still have debates with each other and with senior management, but that these interactions are healthier and more constructive than in the years Gates and his successor Steve Ballmer ran the company. At the same time, Gates and Ballmer deserve great credit for recognizing that the company needed a different type of leader in its post-founder era, and they found it in Nadella. Similarly, one has the strong impression from watching Gates in videos and in reading his blog that he has mellowed in his new role, together with Melinda, as two of the world's greatest philanthropists.

Likewise, Tim Cook has done at Apple what few thought possible after Jobs's death, and promoted continued innovation in the various i-products, with a team-oriented culture similar to that of its once main rival in personal computing operating systems, Microsoft (the two companies have since changed their business models so much that they are no longer exclusively competing head-to-head).

The importance of a team-oriented culture has been recognized outside of tech, not just in start-ups or young firms but also in well established companies. Novartis, one of the world's leading drug companies, is an example. Since taking the reins of the company in early 2017, Vas Narasimhan, a former HIV/AIDS and malaria researcher and one-time McKinsey consultant, has been working to radically transform the corporate culture from one of top-down management, the tradition throughout Big Pharma, to a bottom-up culture centered on teamwork among scientists who are well below top management. As he explained to *Fortune* in 2018, Narasimhan believes "the future of companies is going to be about ideas coming from the bottom up. . . . We don't need bosses. We need servant leaders. We need people to serve their teams and let their teams come up with the best ideas."[16] In this boss-less work environment, scientific teams are encouraged to take risks and to move away from the company's prior perfectionist culture. Although there is nothing explicit in Narasimhan's organizational pivot about welcoming debate, that is the inevitable feature of any teamwork-centered culture."[17]

Though it may appear so on the surface, a healthy debate work culture is not inconsistent with one that values teamwork. To the contrary, only when workers and their supervisors feel part of the same team are team members likely to feel safe to take the risks associated with advocating a point of view that might differ from others on the team. In any group or organizational setting, the best ideas are most likely to emerge through a healthy process of give-and-take, which debate promotes. This happens only when ideas or arguments are depersonalized so that, after contentious discussion, participants can walk away with their friendships or work-related bonds intact.

Les Lynn told me a story from his years on the highly competitive national high school debate circuit that underscores the lessons of depersonalizing arguments that debate teaches. To save travel costs, out-of-town team members at major tournaments often would be placed with host families in the cities where tournaments were held, and often these families were those of competing debaters. Because high school debate can be an all-consuming activity, debaters whose families host these guests often hang out and became friendly with their rivals, bonding with each other, almost paradoxically, through their intense and competitive commitment to rhetoric and evidence-based argument, all the while knowing that, should they meet in a tournament round, they must vigorously compete with one another. That lesson from competitive debate—being able to separate arguments from the personalities making them—is central to the success of teams that are devoted to reaching a common goal and where the members are not in competition with each other.

Creating a debate-oriented company culture is something that can come only from the top, most likely the CEO and his or her top executives. If they do not set the tone themselves for separating ideas from those who advocate for or against them—and welcome the give-and-take that debaters are trained for—then there is no way lower level employees who have debate training can instill that kind of culture in the companies they work for. If they try, they are likely to be fired or marginalized—or just as likely, not want to work for companies that do not value their abilities.

As more students gain debate training—in the classroom or in competitive settings—before they become adults and join the workforce, the more likely it will be that, over time, more organizations will adopt debate-friendly cultures. In that way, a virtuous cycle will take hold, which can benefit not only employees and their employers but the entire economy.

Debate Training Would Benefit Workers in the Twenty-First Century Workforce

One day in May 2019, the *Wall Street Journal* devoted a section of its paper to advice for college graduates that year.[18] It explained that because software has taken over many routine back-office tasks, employers want graduates who will step in to help them right away, not simply shadow existing workers or spend time in company training programs. What kinds of skills satisfy these immediate demands?

The article mentioned four in particular: the ability to communicate directly with those inside and outside the firm, the ability to listen carefully to the needs of clients and fellow employees, analytical skills (especially facility with the many functions of Excel software), and adaptability (the ability to continuously learn new skills). Apart from the technical skills cited in the article, its focus on the importance of "social skills" in the labor market is consistent with recent economic literature.[19] The items on the list are also consistent with the kinds of skills referred to in chapter 4 that educators say students will need in the twenty-first century.

Notice anything about the *Wall Street Journal* list? The first two items—communications and listening skills—are precisely the skills that debate, in the classroom and in competition, teaches and hones. Yet today, probably less than 1 percent of graduating college seniors, and surely a lower percentage of community college and high school graduates, have had any kind of formal debate training. This fact is consistent with the findings of a survey of workers of different ages reported on in the same article, that asked this question: "Thinking about your own experiences, how well did your academic experience prepare you for the workforce?" Of the people over sixty-five, obviously raised and educated in a much earlier time (much like me), 81 percent answered "very well" or "somewhat well." In contrast, among younger people, or those in the eighteen to thirty-four age group, 73 percent provided the same response, a difference of eight percentage points. The disparity by age was even greater among those who gave only a "very well" response: 38 percent among seniors to just 28 percent among the younger group, a difference of 10 percentage points. In other words, young workers today know that their formal education is doing a poorer job of preparing them for a rapidly changing workforce, yet our educators—in college and well before that—are not doing the best they can to provide two of the four most important skills employers now say they want in new hires.

Communications and other related skills are important not only for today's college graduates. A 2018 survey of 1,000 employers seeking to hire MBA graduates put communication skills at the top of the list of skills and abilities these employers were seeking.[20] Even high school educated applicants for entry level jobs—whether in fast food, retail, or manufacturing—have a leg up on getting hired, and certainly on moving up, if they listen well and can speak clearly and thoughtfully, the same two skills valued among college graduates, skills that formal debate training develops.

Debate training also should have positive impacts extending well beyond students' first or second jobs. Instilling a positive attitude toward learning should be the central purpose of education, especially in this age of the Internet, when facts and all kinds of educational materials are available—for free!—through search engines and multiple websites (check out the Khan Academy's website, www.khanacademy. org/, where you can learn or re-learn just about anything). Debate's greatest value, thus, may not be just the communications, thinking, and research skills it develops but the fact that it teaches students both how to learn and that the process of learning—teaching themselves—can be fun.

The importance of this desire-for-learning mindset cannot be over-stated, especially in this age of "automation anxiety," when it is widely feared that human beings will, increasingly, be replaced by machines, especially machines enabled by software that "thinks" or learns on its own, or artificial intelligence (AI). Contrary to the pessimists who worry that the AI revolution will create mass unemployment—leading some to call for a "universal basic income" presumably because so much work will be made obsolete by software and robots—other jobs will be created as automation advances, just as has happened throughout American history and in other economies as well. Among other positive employment effects, the cost savings generated by AI will be spent on *other* goods and services—health care, education, leisure, travel and entertainment—that will need more people to make and deliver them. In addition, policymakers can use fiscal and monetary policies to boost aggregate demand sufficiently to assure full or close to full employment.[21]

There are two very real problems associated with AI and automation, however, which explains why one survey suggests that over 70 percent of Americans are "worried" that it will cause joblessness.[22] The first and obvious downside is that transitions are painful: workers whose jobs cannot somehow by augmented by AI or software (think, for example, of anyone who works with a word processor) or robotics but are, instead, replaced by these technologies, must find new jobs or careers, which entails income loss during unemployment and may require moving to another location. Americans have been gradually less willing or able to move in recent decades, in part because locations where jobs are plentiful typically have higher costs of living, especially housing.

The second downside of technological advance is related to the first: whether workers stay or move, they may have to take a cut in wages or salary (totally independent of any higher living costs in a new locale), whose effects may be permanent. This effect is analogous to falling a step or two down a ladder and not being able to climb back up.

Compounding the transition problem, automation favors workers who have skills developing or using computers and information technologies, which allows them to increase their productivity and incomes at a faster rate than workers without these skills.[23] As economist Harry Holzer has noted, this "skill-biased technical change" is the main force driving increased income inequality,[24] which Stanford economist and former chair of the Council of Economic Advisers Ed Lazear attributes to the productivity gap in the United States and other advanced countries between workers at the top of the income distribution and those below them.[25] For example, most growth in GDP since the 1960s has benefited those in the top half of the income distribution, especially those at the very top, the highest-earning 1 percent.[26] With income distribution becoming more polarized, aggravated by income and wealth disparities between large urban areas and smaller cities and rural areas,[27] it is no surprise that the same polarization is reflected in our politics.

Ultimately, the best way to narrow the productivity gap between people at different points along the income distribution is to narrow their skills gap by enhancing the marketable skills of those whose current earnings put them in the lower and middle parts of the income distribution. Government policy has an important role to play to help achieve this objective. The federal government should offer a combination of income-contingent loans (whose repayment is tied to workers' future incomes) and grants for lifetime learning,[28] while providing wage insurance to partially make up for the drop in workers' wages caused by disruptive change, whatever the cause. Wage insurance is a policy measure advocated by various Brookings authors, including myself throughout most of my professional career, with not much success, although the idea has been attracting more attention in the academic and policymaking communities.[29]

This is not to say that better education and lifetime training—what entrepreneur and venture capitalist Nick Hanauer calls "educationism"—are the magic cures for the increase in inequality. In a thoughtful 2019 essay in *The Altantic*, Hanauer argues that the major cause of inequality now and in the future is *preexisting* inequality—

namely, that your odds of doing well in school and later in life are heavily determined by the income of the family into which you were born and raised.[30] Accordingly, rising inequality will not be reversed, in his view—in which he has plenty of company—until society mounts a massive transfer of income to those with lower and middle incomes. One means of doing this is to expand the earned income tax credit (EITC) in a major way. Higher minimum wages also would narrow income differentials, though the higher the floor the greater will be the adverse impact on unemployment.

More progressive taxation or higher minimum wages, however, should not rule out the adoption of teaching innovations, such as DCI, that will better equip students, especially those from low income families, with skills that will help make them more economically successful throughout their adult lives.

As for adult workers confronting continuing demands for different kinds of workplace skills, the challenge to acquire and master new skills is not easy, nor is the mindset to want to do that easy to instill or cultivate. People generally dislike or, dare I say, even hate insecurity, especially economic insecurity. But in our world today, most people who want a rising standard of living through their lifetimes must acquire, in the words of author John Lancaster, an "education that prepares them for a lifelong process of training and retraining. They will need, more than anything else, *to learn how to learn*" (emphasis added).[31]

Ideally, government policies will help workers finance the acquisition of new skills. My Brookings colleague Richard Reeves, who heads up a continuing research project on developing ways to restore the middle class, has been quoted as wanting to "see more apprenticeships or 'returnships' for workers who need to learn new skills. Colleges could include more programming and scholarship money for adult learners. Or we could change our credentialing system so that credits are more easily transferable or can be accrued from work experience. Then, workers would be able to take a few classes at different institutions and, over time, combine those credits to get a certification or diploma."[32]

It doesn't take sophisticated statistical analysis, just a modest dose of common sense, to realize that adults who were bored in school and, thus, turned off by learning when they were young are less likely to want to learn these new skills, let alone train for new careers, than those who enjoyed or were challenged by learning in school. The education literature makes clear that students are more excited about learning when they are engaged in learning, which is why project-based learning is making such headway across the United States. As emphasized in the previous chapter, debate and argument-based pedagogy is just another form of PBL, except that the "projects" are the everyday subjects or units that are taught in school now. DCI can help instill the mindset in students that learning can be fun and engaging while showing them, as Lancaster emphasizes, how to learn.

One study of competitive debaters in Chicago's Urban Debate League published in 2019 demonstrates that students engaged in that activity show statistically significant gains in noncognitive skills, such as "grit," relative to nondebaters.[33] Although students benefitting from DCI will not receive as heavy a dose of debate training, the skills are similar, and so it is plausible to infer that they, too, will be more motivated to learn than they would be otherwise. That, in turn, is why it stands to reason that the mindset benefits of debate or argument-centered instruction in high school should help address workers' anxiety about their economic futures.

The mindset benefits of debate will be especially important in the twenty-first century labor market, and likely beyond. Through much of the twentieth century, most people's work careers were "straight," in the sense that, whether in agriculture, manufacturing, or service jobs, people either were schooled for certain professional occupations (accountants, lawyers, doctors, and so on) or learned certain skills on the job with one or few employers, and they pretty much remained in their occupations most or all of their working lives.

That is no longer true for many, if not most, workers, and it surely will not be true in the rest of this century as continuing changes in technology make many jobs and occupations obsolete while creating new ones. Most economists (me included) believe, with much historical evidence to back this up, that so long as macroeconomic policies maintain growth in aggregate demand for goods and services and match the combined growth of the labor force and productivity, the new jobs, which admittedly will require new training, will be filled. No one knows with any confidence, however, whether the incomes attached to those jobs will grow to be more or less equal than they are today.

One thing, though, about this century's labor market is already clear: many, if not most, career paths will be "crooked"—not in the sense of being corrupt or illegal, but because people will voluntarily change or be compelled to change jobs and occupations to fit the constantly changing skill demands of employers. The not-so-straight but highly successful career paths of two very different individuals will be a lot more typical of careers in the twenty-first century than in the previous one.

Consider first the life story (so far) of Arthur Brooks, who grew up wanting to be a French horn player; not just any French horn musician, but the *best in the world.*[34] He diligently practiced his craft when he was young, dropped out of college at the age of nineteen to play professionally, hoping, as he has said, to "keep rising through the classical-music ranks," playing for symphony orchestras.

But then in his twenties, for some reason he still cannot explain, Brooks' playing ability topped out and even began to regress. He describes a pivotal moment when he literally fell off the stage during a concert as he was about to perform at Carnegie Hall in New York. Nonetheless, he continued to struggle in the music business until late in his twenties, when he realized he better earn a college degree after all—just in case the "music thing" never worked out—and he did, through distance learning (today it would be called online), by the age of thirty, while still scraping up the rent as a French hornist.

Brooks's career ascendancy after that has been truly remarkable. He went on to gain a Ph.D. in public policy analysis, which opened doors to academia and relatively soon thereafter to a professorship at Syracuse University. By his early forties, he was considered such an academic star that one of the nation's other leading think tanks, the American

Enterprise Institute (AEI, now located two doors away from the Brookings Institution), made him its president, where he had a hugely successful decade-long run before joining the faculty at age fifty-five of Harvard's Kennedy School of Government as professor of the practice of public leadership.

Brooks had no formal debate training in high school and told me he was very nervous about public speaking well into thirties. But like learning to play the French horn, he practiced his speeches extensively before giving them. He said he even used to practice before "murder boards" of his colleagues—which is close to what competitive debaters do much earlier in their lives—while he was AEI president as a way of preparing to deliver his talks. It has paid off—showing it is never too late to acquire, through hard practice, the persuasive speaking skills that the best kinds of debate foster. Brooks today is an outstanding public speaker, as well as a prolific author, having written eleven books, two of them *New York Times* best sellers.

Then there is the remarkable career U-turn of Nkechi Okuro Carroll, the youngest of four children of Nigerian parents. She was born in New York City, then was moved back to Nigeria and later to the Ivory Coast by her parents, who divorced just before Nkechi's eighth birthday.[35] Nkechi was fortunate enough to attend boarding school in Oxford, England, where she developed an interest in literature and performing in the Oxford Youth Theatre. On the strength of her accomplishments and unusual background, Nkechi was accepted to the University of Pennsylvania and graduated in three years in economics and French. She wrote short stories and plays in her "spare time," honing creative skills she would use later in life.

But after finishing school, getting a secure paycheck was her priority, and her economics degree provided just the ticket. The Federal Reserve Bank of New York hired her as a trader/analyst. The job paid the bills, but it didn't satisfy her creative side. At night, after work, Nkechi took acting classes, showed up at TV auditions, and even put on plays in small theaters (acting entails similar speaking and performance skills as debate, and in high school has competitions like debate does). But what she really wanted to do was to write television shows, so also in her "spare time," she taught herself to write TV scripts by downloading scripts of her favorite TV shows from the Internet.

Six years after graduating, she and her husband took the plunge and moved to Hollywood, hoping Carroll would connect her way into a TV script writing job. Mindful of the need for a paycheck, however, she worked days at the Los Angeles branch of the Federal Reserve Bank of San Francisco, while networking with as many people connected to television shows and writing as she could.

Her hard work in her spare hours eventually paid off. After eight years in Los Angeles, Nkechi landed her first TV writing job on *The Finder*, a Fox drama that was spun off from the highly successful show *Bones*. With that break, Nkechi quit her day job at the Fed and launched an entirely new career, which has taken off like a rocket ship.

Nkechi later moved to a writing position on *Bones* itself, and then to similar positions, including producing roles on two other television shows, before signing a multi-year contract with Warner Brothers to generate her own shows, while serving as a writer for its show *All American*. In October 2018, Nkechi was promoted to showrunner for that *All American*—effectively head writer and producer at the same time—the top off-screen job one can have in television.

Few of us have the intellectual or creative talents of remarkable people like Brooks or Carroll. But everyone has some innate skills they can develop, refine, and derive personal and financial satisfaction from, if they have the right mindset and opportunities. My claim here is simply that debate training in high school, and even earlier, increases the odds that everyone who receives it will gain the mindset they will need to have psychologically and financially rewarding careers, whatever they decide to do.

Ideally, government policies would be in place to help finance people who want to seize those opportunities, not just during the K–12 and college years, but throughout people's working lives. Until they are, the challenges in retraining for new jobs, and possibly new occupations, will be far more difficult for far too many than they should be. But that only means that the mindset skills that debate facilitates will be even more important in the years ahead until government policies change.

SIX

Objections and Challenges to Debate-Centered Instruction

The notion that students can and should learn through argumentation is not common sense to everyone. In the late 1990s, author Deborah Tannen made a powerful case that we had, then, too much argumentation in society, and thus, by implication, her thesis would have opposed the kind of DCI I have advocated for use in high school and middle school classes. This chapter begins by laying out Tannen's well-argued (pun partially intended) case and then shows why it shouldn't derail movement toward more instruction through argumentation.

The chapter then turns to a series of challenges that a broad-based effort to instill DCI across the school curriculum throughout the country is likely to face. In each case, I explain why these challenges can be overcome. The political challenge of persuading local educational authorities—principally school board and superintendents—to adopt DCI is left for the concluding chapter.

Rebutting the Case against Argument-Centered Learning

Given the political polarization we see today, Deborah Tannen wrote a remarkably prescient book in 1998, *The Argument Culture: Stopping America's War of Words*, which predicts much of what has happened since and, as her title suggests, lays the blame on what she sees as our excessively argumentative culture. She found then, and certainly there is ample evidence that things have gotten worse over the past two decades, too much argumentation on television, in Congress, and between the White House and the press and vice versa. Tannen's book contains various examples of how our society rewards argumentation, confrontation, and attack rather than compromise and the search for truth. She even makes a compelling case that our legal system, which is inherently argumentative and confrontational, does not do a great job uncovering the truth, a conclusion echoed in a recent comprehensive critique of the U.S. criminal justice system advanced by criminologist John Pfaff.[1]

Tannen also correctly noted that, as discussed in chapter 3, there are some issues where there are no two "good" sides—the existence of slavery in the United States (and in other countries) and of the Holocaust are obvious examples—while on many other issues there are multiple sides because the problems are complex and solutions necessarily require some compromise. The main thesis of her book resonates even more strongly in our time, more than twenty years later.

How then can anyone now be urging that our children need more skills in argumentation? Won't that further aggravate and divide the country? Similar objections have been lodged by some teachers.[2]

If implemented in the wrong way, debate-centered education certainly would have that effect. But that is not what is advocated throughout this book, nor how DCI is typically delivered. Unlike the talking heads or fixtures on cable TV who are the villains, among others, in *Tannen's* book, and who mix ad hominem, personalized attacks with occasional dollops of substance, competitive and classroom debate teaches students that there is room for respectful disagreement on most subjects and how to express that disagreement in the most persuasive way. Chapter 3 certainly acknowledges that there are some subjects that should be off limits to debate in school but asserts that those limits should be determined at the local level.

Chapter 3 also notes that teaching through argumentation allows for many different points of view on many subjects, so long as students make the logical and evidentiary case for their claims. For example, most wars have multiple causes, and there are multiple theories about why dinosaurs became extinct. Teaching by argumentation is designed to elicit from the students themselves, based on materials compiled by the teacher and, ideally, also through additional research by students themselves, the evidence backing these multiple causes or theories. Debate or argument-centered learning does not have to be, nor should it be, restricted just to "two sides," which is one of Tannen's main worries.

Tannen's critique of "both sides" argumentation also has been eclipsed by the evolution of competitive policy debate, which has allowed the affirmative side to take the best features of a negative team's counterplan to revise the affirmative's initial plan by offering a permutation and then claim that it is even better than the counterplan—a mode of argument that can be difficult to rebut. Putting aside the winning advantages of this perm strategy, introduced in chapter 2, the back-and-forth discussion of plans to address the chosen debate topic is precisely the kind of multi-sided conversation Tannen believes we need to foster. The structures of other forms of competitive high school debate, such as PF debate (where the topics change regularly), LD debate (one person per side), or parliamentary debate are not as flexible as for policy debate: There are no counterplans or perms. But since the emphasis is more on persuasion than rapid speaking skills, there is more room for creativity and less for pure argumentation of the kinds one sees on cable TV.

Trish Hall, the former op-ed editor of the *New York Times* offers a variation of the Tannen critique in her book *Writing to Persuade*, which also (perhaps unintentionally) provides several solutions that comport with the kind of instruction advocated here.[3] Hall's critique of argumentation will strike a chord with many readers from their own life experience: "Most of the time, if you argue, you will annoy people and make them feel battered and defensive (or worse, bore them). The person you're trying to convince will also argue, voices will get louder, and a standoff will ensue. Ever watch two drivers argue? I'm always worried that physical violence is the next step."

Hall admits there is an exception to the implication of this statement, by allowing "if you're in a situation that calls for [argument]: *a college debate,* a pro and a con on a certain subject on a panel" (emphasis added). Teaching through debate techniques in high school or earlier would seem to fit within Hall's exception, because it has a structure to it that, for reasons already outlined, should improve students' acquisition and retention of knowledge, as well as reasoning and speaking skills—virtues that should benefit them when they grow up to be workers and voters.

Fortunately, Hall goes on to suggest ways of persuading others that do not run the risks of offending and creating the downward spiral of defensiveness and anger she posits at the beginning. Admittedly, her suggestions are confined to ways of writing, but they apply with equal force to speaking and all attempts to persuade others or to try to open (if not change) their minds.

First, she urges writers (and speakers, I would say) to avoid personal attacks and, instead, to focus on ideas. Second, she urges people to "concede the good points of the other side," a technique that is likely to defuse tension and make other people more likely to accept what you have to say. Third, in a related point, she counsels people to "show respect for the other person's opinion," advice that is likely to have a similar positive effect. Both competitive debate and DCI in the classroom adhere to and, indeed, instill in their participants all three of these principles.

Hall's final suggestion, citing social science research that people are not likely to be persuaded by facts, is that writers (and speakers) make their points by telling stories or anecdotes, which she argues are much more compelling and more likely to be remembered. There clearly is some truth to this, but the persuasiveness of stories is not inconsistent with the claim-evidence-reasoning paradigm on which all rational thought is based and which is at the heart of DCI. Students and adults need to pay attention to facts and how they do or do not support a claim, and to understand this basic connection, because that it is key to how they will adapt to and, ideally, change for the better the world they will enter as adults.

Of course, it may continue to be true that, in a hypothetical society populated by people who have had formal debate training, stories still will resonate better than facts. If so, then successful debating requires some amount of story-telling, though compressed, given the limited time people generally have to make their points.

In the end, the precise nature of argumentation doesn't matter in one important respect. Debates, whether in competitive tournaments or in the classroom, necessarily engage participants in thinking about what the other side has to say and why their side might be weak. You're not usually going to win such a debate unless you understand the other side better than the opponents do. When you get to that point, you'll know the weaknesses of your own positions and be more open-minded, as well. That outcome is one to be welcomed and encouraged, and is one that DCI is designed to achieve.

Overcoming Potential Challenges to Widespread Adoption of DCI

Broader implementation of DCI faces several challenges, some that have been explicitly made and others that must be anticipated, because this mode of instruction has not been on the agenda of many school reformers or educational authorities to date. Certain of these challenges help explain why DCI has not been more universally implemented. Nonetheless, there are answers to each of these challenges. With enough will, all can be overcome.

Insufficient Support from Debate and
Speech Teachers (Not a Concern)

Ironically, forensics and speech teachers—who typically double as debate coaches and often teach other subjects, such as history, civics, or English—so far have not been interested in developing ways to introduce debate techniques in other subjects. Lynn reports certain exceptions, such as Tara Tate, the former director of debate at Glenbrook South High School, who was a successful competitive debate coach and who developed and taught argument-based learning strategies at her school, and David Baker, former director of debate at St. Mark's School in Dallas, Texas, who did something similar. But these teachers are still the exceptions and not the rule.

In part, debate and speech teachers have not generally embraced DCI because they may be unaware of how DCI can be, and already is being, used in certain classrooms and how they could play an important role in facilitating the implementation of DCI in their own schools. In addition, many debate coaches—often the good ones—are perfectly happy coaching their small but elite groups of students and may not be interested in or have the time to expand their workloads (even if paid extra to do so) to train and oversee other teachers to use argument-based teaching techniques in a broad range of nonspeech-related classroom settings.

Fortunately, as both Lynn in Chicago and the BDL in Boston have shown, DCI can be taught to subject matter teachers without the active participation of speech and debate teachers, although involving the latter group in DCI training would be helpful. To be clear, debate- or argument-centered instruction in most classrooms is somewhat different than the specialized training one finds in a class devoted entirely to speech and debate. DCI typically calls for short, frequent presentations and responses and questions that are much different in character than the typical initial presentations and rebuttals—all of which are found in various types of competitive debate. The subject matter content taught in the multiple units in classrooms also differs from the typical policy-oriented resolutions that focus competitive debates.

For all these reasons, and probably more, teaching with debate-based techniques is different from teaching or coaching competitive debate. Lynn and the BDL, nonetheless, have shown that teachers can be trained in the basics of DCI in about a week—by individuals with some debate background, but not necessarily the debate teacher in a school—and then coached throughout the school year by the same individuals. This training model can be scaled, by having teachers who have used DCI in their classrooms for a year or two serve as the trainers for other teachers in the school.

Of course, those speech and debate teachers who want to serve as instructors and coaches for other teachers using debate techniques in their classrooms should be welcomed with open arms. At the same time, because coaching competitive debate requires major commitments of time and energy from the debate coaches, principals should not press these teachers to become involved in DCI training and coaching if they don't volunteer. My educated guess, however, is that once DCI gets going in a school and proves successful, more speech and debate teachers, many of whom are competitive by nature (directly, from their own pasts, or through their students who are competitive debaters) will want to get involved.

Many Teachers May Not Want DCI Initially

Many subject matter teachers may reject DCI, at least initially, and it is not hard to understand why. In many states, teachers' salaries haven't kept up with inflation, which has led to teacher strikes, with some limited wage gains, in some surprising "red" states—Arizona, Oklahoma, and West Virginia, among others. One silver lining of the horrible COVID-19 pandemic is that parents who were forced by school closures to supervise the home schooling of their children gained a greater appreciation of the value of teachers and may be more willing in the future, as taxpayers, to support higher teacher pay. Even so, more money is unlikely to quell the worries that teachers have about their own safety and that of their students in the wake of so many active shootings in places that were once deemed safe.

So even if they saw debate-centered education as a way for making teaching duties easier and classrooms more exciting learning environments, a natural reaction of some teachers to being required or even just encouraged to incorporate DCI methods, understandably could be to say, in effect, "I've had it. I can't take any more change, especially if I'm not being paid extra to do it."

Other teachers may worry that they don't have the creativity or spontaneity to teach the way DCI demands. Teachers used to being the sage on the stage and answering a few questions from students may feel uncomfortable or even marginalized if they are seemingly "demoted" to the role of walking around the classroom and coaching the students in multiple small groups who grapple with the claim-evidence-reasoning-rebuttal mode of learning demanded by DCI. These teachers may fear that if they allow their students to debate the material, they might lose control of their classrooms to especially industrious students who may discover, through their outside research, information that the teachers themselves don't know. Or they may feel compelled to check that information themselves, a step some teachers may believe exposes their limitations to their students.

Still other teachers who otherwise would be open to experimenting with new teaching methods could, nonetheless, reject DCI because of the unfavorable perception (albeit one that can be fixed) that many have of debate from watching unstructured political "debates" on nightly television shows, especially cable TV. Or teachers who have watched in person or on YouTube the speed debating that is common at competitive debate tournaments may incorrectly equate all debating with that style. Understandably, if these images of debating are the sole examples of what debate-centered instruction would look like, few teachers would want to introduce it into their classrooms.

Other teachers may be philosophically skeptical or downright opposed to having students debate both or multiple sides of issues they personally believe are already well settled—immigration, climate change, the role of capitalism, or what have you. In other words, this group of teachers has philosophical leanings—left or right—that they want to make sure to transmit to their students, though subtly to be sure. For these teachers, opening their own views to debate is something they may not want to do.

Then there is the fact that introducing DCI into classroom settings is, at least initially, demanding work. It not only requires assembling packets of assigned materials that serve as the evidence students will seek out to support claims, but in the classrooms themselves effective DCI instruction requires hands-on coaching of individual students or small groups. These functions require different skill sets from delivering lesson plans in a lecture format. Not all teachers will be good at DCI, at least not without initial instruction and coaching throughout the first year or two from more experienced practitioners.

All of these objections are understandable, which is the reason they are summarized here. To those teachers who initially or permanently don't want to use DCI techniques in their classrooms, fine. DCI should be adopted only voluntarily, even in schools where the principals are strongly in favor of it; where principals are opposed, DCI just won't happen while they are there (which is not forever, because there is turnover among principals in schools).

However, I am optimistic that many superintendents, principals, and teachers will want to try DCI for all the reasons laid out throughout this book: it just makes so much sense. The more people—policymakers, parents, and students—who realize the potential power of DCI, the more support it will attract. All it takes is for more DCI experiments to begin. Once that happens, enthusiasm for DCI will grow. Initial impressions change over time, as teachers who find DCI a valuable, even essential, addition to their teaching techniques spread the word to other teachers, in their own schools and beyond.

Perhaps the most powerful mind-changer is for schools to host a "debate" or "argument-centered education" week, in which both teachers who use and don't use the techniques observe each other's classrooms, and then meet during one or more professional development sessions to trade their findings. When teachers who don't initially embrace DCI see its power with their own eyes—in particular, the high level of student engagement and energy—in classrooms, they are more likely to try it themselves. That's what I saw with my own eyes during visits to schools in Boston and Chicago that use DCI in the classroom.

Indeed, the BDL itself got into the business of training teachers in evidence-based argumentation in the Boston public schools through the "eye test," that is being witnessed by an individual who had the ability to make things happen. In 2012, then Boston school superintendent Carol Johnson attended the championship round of the debate tournament of schools belonging to the Boston Urban Debate League, which the BDL at the time had exclusively concentrated on assisting. Johnson was so impressed with the quality of the debate and the debaters that she asked the BDL to assist the entire school district to implement debate broadly into other classes.

As discussed in chapter 3, after initial difficulties doing precisely that, the BDL came up, independently, with a model similar to the one Lynn was using in Chicago, by using evidence-based argumentation as a pedagogical technique for teaching the same material teachers were then delivering mostly through standard lecture formats. This approach required some training and ongoing coaching but did not require students to take a separate speech and debate class to learn argumentation skills, which meant that its version of DCI did not detract from teaching other material; instead, it became the vehicle for teaching the same material teachers were already required to cover, but in a different and more compelling way.

Won't Debate Disadvantage Some Students?

Even those who don't stutter, like I did as a child, can be shy or even afraid about speaking up in class. Do an internet search for "fear of public speaking" and you'll see links claiming it to be the worst fear that most people have, even greater than the fear of death for some. Why subject the masses of students to the pain and humiliation of that exercise? A related objection can be raised about subjecting children whose native language is not English to similar obstacles.

I worried about these objections when I began research for this book, and I wasn't sure how those with day-to-day experience with DCI handled these issues. After my visits to the schools in Boston and Chicago that use DCI in the classroom, my fears were put at ease. Readers who harbor similar concerns should also put them aside. Here's why.

Training in argument-centered learning starts gradually, typically with the classroom being split into groups of four to six individuals. This allows shy or ESL students to speak before smaller groups without the fear of embarrassing themselves before an entire class. Other forms of argument-based instruction, as discussed in chapter 3, are designed to put the fun in learning while not putting students "on the spot" to speak until they are ready. As noted earlier, teachers in both cities using variations of DCI are supportive of students' efforts to make their points, however imperfectly, which creates an atmosphere of positivity. Rather than telling a student that her answer is "wrong," teachers ask the rest of each group or the entire class something like "Does anyone else have a *different* answer?" This is important, because young people who lack confidence in their ability to speak or to speak in English, need a welcoming environment, not one that will shut them down.

It works. Melissa Graham, who teaches ESL classes at the Lilla G. Frederick Pilot Middle School in Boston, has students speaking as many as five different native languages. By welcoming all ideas and arguments in her classroom, she reports that even the most reluctant students come out of their shells. Starting with just one or two sentences stated as a claim, a recitation of evidence from her supporting materials, or a reason why the evidence supports the claim, she enables her students to build up their critical thinking and speaking abilities over time.

Graham helps this process along by giving students choices about what roles in an argument they want to play. In increasing order of difficulty, these choices might include an opening statement, like the first affirmative speech in a competitive debate round, which can be written out and memorized or delivered from notes; a closing statement, which requires synthesizing prior arguments but allows students to process and organize what they hear; and the most difficult speaking parts in between, namely providing reasons why evidence supports the claim, or responses that question the evidence and/or the reasoning. Graham finds that students who begin with the easier roles and develop confidence in mastering them tend to move on to the more difficult ones, just as everyone does in school or at any task if they are motivated to do so. Debates in the classroom can provide just that sort of motivation in school settings.

Moreover, Graham finds that as her students gain confidence in their abilities to speak persuasively, their voices grow louder, a sign of confidence. By the end of a semester, each student is able, literally, to get up on a "soapbox"—which Graham constructs specially for her classes—and make a reasoned argument. Graham reports examples of ESL students who begin the school year struggling with English who are, by the end, sometimes well equipped to be mainstreamed with native English-speaking students.

Being assertive and able to speak up for themselves is important to ESL students, in the classroom and in real life, Graham stresses. The parents of many of these students must deal with various government agencies, especially those related to housing and immigration, just to survive in this country. With limited speaking abilities of their own, these parents are grateful to have their children be their advocates in these situations.[4]

Lynn has tried a different approach with certain teachers who have students whose native language is Spanish. He encourages these teachers to hold argument-centered exercises with these students in their native tongue at the outset of a semester, to build confidence just in their ability to speak, before asking these students to participate gradually in English versions of the same or different exercises. Lynn reports success with this approach.

I have no strong views whether conducting debate-centered activities in a student's native language as a jump starter to doing them in English or just immersing them in English-only training at the outset is superior. This is a decision that should be up to the school principal or even individual teachers. Both can work, although the BDL mentors note that academic learning in one's native language supports second-language acquisition. The BDL has a debate *en español* league for competitive debate. The Margarita Muñiz Academy in Boston is a dual language school, and evidence-based argumentation is implemented in both English and Spanish.

Lynn also addresses concerns that native English-speaking students may be reluctant to speak up out of fear that they may be wrong and potentially face humiliation in front of their peers. Some prefer to remain quiet because they know they are not as proficient in making arguments as others who have better speaking skills. Lynn counsels that teachers should elicit from the more fearful students suggestions they may have for how other better-speaking students might improve their arguments. In the process, both types of students should benefit. The more reserved students can develop confidence knowing they have something to contribute even if they aren't initially as proficient as others in the class. And the better-speaking students can profit by learning how to explain their points in ways that everyone can understand—a lesson that will serve them (and others) well in all kinds of settings when they are adults.

My own personal experience recounted earlier in this chapter illustrates how someone with not only a fear of speaking but an inability to speak properly can overcome that fear through debate. Many psychologists believe the best way for someone to conquer any fear or source of anxiety is to gradually expose themselves to that fear as a way of inoculating against the instinctive fight-or-flight response. If introduced the right way, in baby steps, beginning with one-on-one sessions with teachers and then gradual exposure to larger audiences, forensics training coupled with student's desire for competition should get most over their fear of speaking, let alone arguing in a structured manner, which is what debate in any format is all about.

Amity Shlaes, chairman of the Calvin Coolidge Presidential Foundation, which sponsors its own form of persuasive debate, knocks down the claim or perception that debate is only for the select few: "most anyone can debate. I've watched timid teens who don't know how to say 'protectionism' in the morning win a debate on the same subject in the afternoon. As in soccer, football, or sailing an Opti sailboat across a windy bay, *competition in debate causes kids to forget their fears.* The kids learn arguments they never expected to, *both sides*"[5] (emphasis added).

Unexpectedly, remote learning triggered by the pandemic may have made it easier for shy or reluctant students to feel more comfortable speaking to a full classroom of their peers from the comfort of their own rooms through their computers, rather than in person. That conclusion was clear, at least to me, after I had the chance to participate in a Zoom-enabled professional development discussion in mid-April 2020 among Boston teachers who were being trained by the BDL to use DCI techniques online. The BDL facilitators demonstrated how text from a novel could be displayed on students' computer screens and then how the students could be asked to take sides about what the author of the text meant the role of the main character to be and to find "evidence" for their position—just as they would do in a physical classroom. Zoom also allowed the class to be broken down into subgroups and then brought back together, again just as if they were physically in the same room. Ideally something like this exercise would be incorporated at the beginning of each semester in a traditional classroom setting, to make sure that all students feel more comfortable expressing themselves orally from the very beginning before they do so remotely, provided that school districts have the money to ensure that all students have a computer and internet access at home.

Meanwhile, debate—and its virtues—have been recognized even inside prison walls. In 2015, inmates at Eastern New York Correctional Facility in Napanoch, New York, enrolled in a bachelor's degree program offered by Bard College nearby as part of the Bard Prison Initiative (BPI) (see accompanying box) beat a team from Harvard in a competitive debate judged by a panel of neutral judges. In 2019, the same three men beat a British team from Cambridge University that had won one of the top positions that year in a world championship debate competition. The media stories about these events underscore how motivating the

BOX 6-1

The Bard Prison Initiative

The BPI Debate Union typically has about twenty members. Although only three or four people are on stage for each debate, they prepare as a team. The same group of three has never competed together more than once, and the three students who beat Harvard in 2015 all had graduated by the time BPI faced off against Cambridge in 2019. Three different students won that debate.

BPI enrolls students full-time in Bard College degree programs. Academic consistency with the main college campus is important. BPI alumni who have left prison (including those who were on the BPI Debate Union) are now working in a variety of private, nonprofit, and public offices.

preparation for and participation in these debates has been for students pursuing their college degrees inside prison. Not only are people who attend college while incarcerated much less likely to return to prison, they leave with the ambition and tools to create meaningful change for their families and communities. PBS aired a four-part feature about BPI in the fall of 2019.[6] If this initiative doesn't demonstrate the power of debate to change lives, I'm not sure what else will.[7]

The bottom line is this: regardless of a students' initial ability or willingness to speak, or to speak in English, debate-centered education can and should be delivered in a way that enables all students to teach themselves and each other. In this respect, DCI is no different from other things we all learn in life: if we're not exposed to them and try them ourselves, we won't have the chance to learn. Speaking clearly, forcefully, logically—all with confidence—is a skill that is helpful to all people throughout their lives. The sooner they learn it, the better.

How Can Debate Survive in a World Where "Truth" Has Been Challenged?

There are a few pithy quotes I have never forgotten and often use (with proper attribution, of course) in conversation. This one, by former New York senator, Harvard professor, and public intellectual, Daniel Patrick Moynihan, was at the top of my list for many years: "You are entitled to your opinion. But you are not entitled to your own facts."[8]

No more. Today, it seems, people search for their own facts from sources that confirm their beliefs, whether on television (especially cable channels) or on the internet. Social scientists call this confirmation bias. It lies at the heart of our deep political divisions today.

In a world where people believe and hold on to their own facts, there is no objective truth. There is also no way, or even any interest, in separating fact from fiction, "news" from "fake news." Social media aggravates the problem. As writer for *The Atlantic* and Brookings Senior Fellow Jonathan Rauch has noted, false rumors and fake news spread much more rapidly on the internet than accurate reports.

The advertising-based business model of social media rewards this; the more people who click on content, even if it is false or misleading, the more money the platforms make.[9]

Facebook or Twitter each are trying in their own ways to tamp down fake posts, lies, hate speech, and the like on their platforms. But one huge problem with bad content is that far too many actors—including "bots," which account for much of the traffic on the internet—are in on the act. Their messages, however untruthful, are easily amplified by content farms and internet hacks that make money by selling fake content, especially views, or follower accounts to politicians and influencers.

The fake news business will only grow with the ability of literally anyone in their bedroom or garage to "mash" images together and spread misleading or false videos. The implications are beyond dangerous. Videos of world leaders mouthing hateful or dangerous messages made through digital technology to sound just like them could easily set off violence or even wars. Political campaigns in the 2020 election cycle have already used digital distortion technologies to discredit their opponents, and leading AI researchers have worried that they, let alone ordinary citizens, will be unable to keep up with the constantly evolving video fakes.[10]

In this post-truth toxic brew of reality we are all learning how to cope with as adults, how is it possible for teachers to expect their students to debate any subject and to back up their claims with evidence—when trust in once-acceptable sources such as mainstream media publications (on and off-line) and credentialed experts has declined or evaporated?

The answer to this important question is that, at least so far, most of what is taught in school is well accepted and memorialized in textbooks or other functionally equivalent sources. The skepticism over fake news hasn't yet destroyed what is taught in public school classrooms.

That isn't to say there aren't differences of opinion among recognized authorities on a wide range of topics in the humanities and even the sciences. If there weren't, there would be no room for debate. There is no right answer, for example, on why the characters in a novel act the way they do. Historians have always debated, and will continue to do so, over the causes of major events. Are they due to the thoughts and actions of "great men (or women)" or to underlying socioeconomic or demographic trends?

Debate in science also continues over many topics. For example, even though there is a scientific consensus that man-made carbon emissions are contributing to climate change, there are disagreements about the pace and magnitude of these changes and what to do about them—for example, to regulate or tax carbon issues, pursue R&D in renewables, or geo-engineer the atmosphere to reflect sunlight and, thus, at least partially offset the warming effect of the buildup of greenhouse gases.

These are just a few examples of the many topics that can and should be debated in classrooms and taught, not only through sage on the stage lectures but through the kinds of vigorous conversations, and preparation for them, that DCI is designed to foster.

Of course, while most DCI is currently delivered through carefully prepared packets of information, over time more ambitious students will be allowed, even encouraged, to seek out other sources for evidence to back up their claims. This inevitably will lead them to the internet (ideally to the library, as well, but in the wired age, this is unlikely), where truth and falsity mix, with few signposts to help them distinguish between the two. Won't that eventuality undermine efforts to broaden implementation of DCI?

With luck, various fact-checking services will earmark content as reliable or not, even in real time, helping students and adults sort fact from fiction.[11] Teachers should be heavy users of these services. Still, even when perfected, fact-checking services are unlikely to end the war on truth. Multiple fact-checking services will arise that are owned or backed by individuals or organizations with different political leanings. Teachers will need to help their students navigate their way through the maze—helping them debunk truly fake news, understand how to tell when a video is doctored, and learn how to recognize other disinformation techniques—in addition to the research guidance they are already giving to students (for example, how not to stop with Wikipedia entries but to dig deeper, for starters). In some localities, expect political fights over how the teachers, and indeed entire school districts, will be using these web-based fact-checkers, just as there have been fights in some states between creationists or believers in "intelligent design" versus the conventional wisdom of the scientific community that humans and other species have evolved over time through the process of natural selection.

Wider use of DCI techniques will not bring these real-world debates to a halt, though over time they at least may reduce the intensity of fights over hot button issues. Even if that does not happen, the "war on truth" should not prevent the use of DCI in most classroom settings, especially if, as I anticipate, the evidence eventually establishes the positive impact on student learning and engagement that debate in the classroom enables.

In addition, one of the experts consulted in research for this book, David Trigaux, executive direction of the UDL in Washington, D.C., reports that competitive debaters are less likely than nondebaters to share fake news. If so, this suggests that DCI training across the curriculum presumably should have similar effects.

In a Tough Fiscal Environment, How Will
School Districts Pay for DCI?

When I started writing this book, I had assumed that, to prepare students for even the less rigorous forms of debate entailed in DCI, they would all need a one-semester class in basic speech and debate, where rhetoric (the art of persuasion) and logic are also typically taught. I then worried about where already fiscally strapped school districts would be able to find the money—and the teachers with the right qualifications—to teach these courses, assuming school districts would feel comfortable making room in an already crowded school curriculum, presumably in 9th or 10th grade, for a required introductory speech and debate class.

Fortunately, as readers have learned by now, DCI can easily be implemented without such a course and instead in small but gradually more challenging doses in subject matter classes led by teachers without formal speech and debate training. Monies for such training could easily come out of the allocated professional development (PD) funds that now exist in virtually every school district, if the political will is there. One study calculated that, as of 2015, localities were spending an average of $18,000 per teacher annually on PD over nineteen full school days, but only about 30 percent of the teachers improved their performance as a result.[12] Even a two-week summer course in DCI training (say $6,000 maximum, for coaches' fees and residence and travel, if required), coupled with the cost for coaching teachers throughout the year (a job that could be fulfilled by one person, perhaps only part-time) spread across all teachers in a school very likely would cost far less than the total sums spent on PD. If the experiences of the teachers in Chicago and Boston I witnessed first-hand comes even close to being replicated elsewhere, the benefits of DCI-centered professional development training would be far more effective than much (perhaps most) of the training that now exists.

A natural question to ask is who will teach even a one-week summer course for teachers and help them in at least their first year? Even if other school districts want to engage Lynn or Wasserman and his colleagues, for example, they have only so much time and bandwidth. School districts, instead, can turn to those debate coaches who want to volunteer for the effort and use some portion of their current PD funds to pay them. The basic principles for teaching debate techniques for ordinary classroom use are already available on the Argument-Centered Education website, for example.[13] Moreover, as argued earlier, over time many debate coaches are likely to volunteer to coach other teachers in the principles of claim-evidence-reasoning-response. Once they gain experience with DCI, these other teachers, in turn, will be able to teach those principles and act as mentors for succeeding waves of teachers who are hired to teach at their schools.

In short, money should not be a constraint on the implementation of DCI. Moreover, the instructional technique is both replicable and scalable, important features of any reform. In fall 2019, the BDL received a major two-year grant from the Chan Zuckerberg Initiative to develop a classroom observation tool in conjunction with Boston University's School of Education. This tool will help the BDL-assisted schools and teachers improve their own implementation of debate in the classroom and show other school districts how to use the teaching technique as well.

Alleged Political Bias of Debate-Centered Instruction

Another potential objection to debate-centered education draws on another familiar critique of policy debate: that it has a liberal or pro-government bias since the annual policy debate resolution, as well as the rotating resolutions in public forum debate, typically call for "the government" to do something.

At first glance, this pro-government complaint appears to be true, but teams designated to take the negative side of a debate do not have to simply deny the presence or magnitude of the problem the affirmative side posits but show why the plan it proposes won't work. That the rules of policy debate allow negatives to accept the need for change implied by the resolution and then propose their own counterplans explicitly affords debaters the option to offer alternatives that advocate market-like incentives rather than command-and-control solutions that affirmatives typically propose.

In any event, in my interviews I found former debaters were far from monolithic in their own current political views, and without exception all reported that debate had made them more willing to change their minds based on evidence. Policy debate is not inherently politically biased, and certainly the claim-evidence-reasoning paradigm that lies at the heart of the scientific method, and also not so coincidentally at the heart of DCI, does not suffer from political bias either.

Why Implement DCI More Widely When Its Value Hasn't Been Rigorously Confirmed?

This is a legitimate question, and it shouldn't be answered by pointing to other pedagogical reforms or techniques that have been advocated on thin, if any, evidence. Nonetheless, there is more than thin evidence for believing that DCI merits the cautious pace of wider implementation that the political realities in the world of education will permit.

For one thing, we know from chapter 2 that competitive debate—upon which DCI is modeled—has proven educational benefits, even when controlling for self-selection. Moreover, as discussed in chapter 3, the "before-after" experiences with DCI in Boston and Chicago—coupled with my own eyeball observations of schools in those cities—provide highly suggestive, if not presumptive, evidence that broadening the use of DCI throughout high school and middle school, curricula has educational benefits.

There is also much common sense and simply logic supporting the idea. Instruction that substantially reduces the fears that many (perhaps most) students have of public speaking, while giving them the ability and the confidence to articulate their views, should improve their life skills. It also should induce students to look up from their smartphones and communicate with each other by looking at and speaking to them. One reason we see so much hate, name calling, and labeling on social media is that it is easy to write these things while typing on a computer or on a smartphone without having to say these things out loud in front of other people. That would change in a world where students have been socialized and educated from a relatively early age to articulate reasoned positions orally and in a civil way while understanding claims by those who do not agree with you.

DCI also takes advantage of an impulse and desire most students have at an early age to express themselves. DCI, thus, could be viewed as a way of engaging students and their teachers in the fun of learning.

To be sure, more rigorous studies, specifically RCTs, could help confirm these presumptions or, at the very least, help show how DCI as it is currently being practiced can be improved so that its educational and lifetime benefits are clear. A major purpose of this book is to convince the philanthropic community that there is enough presumptive evidence to support these experiments.

But waiting for more scientific "proof" that debate-centered education "works" will mean that millions of students will continue to go through their schooling, or drop out, without gaining the benefits this pedagogical technique is likely to provide. Given the highly decentralized nature of public education in America, even the best documented education-related reform is likely to be adopted at a cautious pace. So, the risks of not going ahead, given the evidence and logic favoring its use, are greater than the risks of not trying to implement the idea until more definitive proof is in.

SEVEN

A Political Roadmap for a
Debate-Centered Educational Revolution

The typical policy oriented book like this one, and virtually all the others I have written in my career, wouldn't have a concluding chapter outlining a political strategy for convincing the relevant decisionmakers—the president, Congress, and regulatory agencies at the federal level, and mayors and governors, city councils, and state legislatures at the local and state levels—to adopt the one or more recommendations outlined by the author. The unstated presumption is that good ideas naturally find their way into policy.

But, of course, that often doesn't happen, or if it does, it may happen years or decades later. When it does, action is often prompted by a crisis, when decisionmakers and their staff are more inclined to look for policy recommendations lying on the proverbial shelf or, in this day and age, hidden in some internet search engine just waiting for the right search words to bring it to light.

Policy analysts and the books and articles they write are judged by their professional peers and often speak only in their discipline's language, which can be unintelligible to the people who, in democratic societies, make decisions by voting. Moreover, too often policy analysts understate the transition costs of moving from the status quo to a new policy environment while ignoring the messy, practical details of how to "sell" their ideas, just as any business must do (yes, the same businesses that economists theorize about), or as any politician at any level of government must do to get elected.

For their part, politicians and their strategists are obsessed with "message" and staying on it while responding to what they think voters will "buy." All too often, the policies recommended by the experts have tradeoffs: they benefit some, often in small amounts that are barely noticed by the beneficiaries, and hurt others, often in large and visible ways. Or the policy they support is likely to promise long-term benefits, which will be appreciated by voters only when they are much older, or by many who are not yet old enough to vote (or maybe unborn), but in the meantime imposes substantial transition costs, more than likely concentrated on classes of firms, workers, and communities.

Princeton's Alan Blinder wrestles with the differences between social scientists and politicians in his book *Advice and Dissent* and points to numerous policies, such as a carbon tax or tradeable emissions and free trade, that illustrate these complications. In the real world, he notes, few policies have only winners and losers. He argues (persuasively, in my view) that politicians tend to use policy analysts more to justify their actions than as guides for what really should be done.[1]

Blinder cites such policies as a carbon tax, tradeable (but capped) emissions, and free trade as examples illustrating these dilemmas or complications. In the real, messy world, few policies generate only winners or have no transition costs. For these reasons, Blinder argues (persuasively, in my view) that politicians tend to use policy analysts to justify what the elected officials believe is in *their* interest—namely, getting reelected—not as guides to what ought to be done.

Not all is hopeless, in Blinder's view, however; it's just that economists and other policy analysts must lower their expectations of the influence they can ever hope to have. Invoking the aspiration of famed British economist John Maynard Keynes, the experts must be content with being the equivalent of dentists (sorry to those few dentists who may be reading this book), useful in emergencies to quell a crisis but not as grand strategists. As for the strategists, Blinder offers some examples where the analysts' technical and limited strategic advice is useful and, not surprisingly, he urges that this advice be taken seriously by the strategists more often.

As an economist and longtime policy analyst, I will try in this concluding chapter to take Blinder's advice to heart. I hope that my arguments in favor of wider adoption of DCI are intelligible to a wide audience, meeting one of Blinder's suggestions. But I want more than that: to provide some thoughts about how to *persuade* key decisionmakers—to some extent state education departments and legislature and governors, but more important, local school boards, superintendents, and principals—to *implement* DCI.

At first blush, it may appear that the instructional changes I recommend are an easier sell than such controversial policies like freer trade or more aggressive policy interventions to mitigate climate change, which have winners who may not realize they've won (some winning only in the very distant future) and some very identifiable losers. In contrast, DCI, if properly and faithfully implemented, should be one of those rare interventions that produce only winners and very few losers.

But this observation doesn't move the ball forward on implementing DCI very far. That is because efforts to persuade relevant decisionmakers to adopt DCI in the classroom confront some very stiff challenges.

For one thing, at bottom, DCI is a pedagogical tool, or a process rather than a substantive innovation, even though I have argued that widespread implementation of DCI would lead to favorable substantive outcomes: improving student performance and engagement (chapter 3), and improved functioning of our democracy (chapter 4), and our workforce (chapter 5). Nonetheless, it is difficult to engage and mobilize others outside the educational system—namely, parents or their children or business leaders—to spend their time and energy on advocating changes in the way those charged with educating, teachers and principals, should be performing their jobs. It would be like customers organizing to try to tell auto companies how to make their cars.

Second, because DCI is a pedagogical reform, it inevitably will compete for time, attention, and money among education professionals with other pedagogical reforms in mind, most of which are better known. The most important of these, as my discussion of the idea in preceding chapters has highlighted, is project-based learning. DCI can and should be viewed as a companion to PBL, for each debate in each classroom requires students to develop and use the research and critical thinking entailed in a "project." But DCI has the additional virtues of developing students' oral communications skills and mindset, something useful to them throughout their adult lives as citizens and as workers and entrepreneurs.

Accordingly, I do not want to be interpreted as casting cold water on other proven pedagogical methods. To the contrary, I say keep them if they work but supplement them with DCI techniques: this is a case where 2 + 2 can equal 5.

Admittedly, many if not most educational leaders already are suffering from "reform fatigue," or "flavor of month" pedagogical proposals. The only way for DCI to survive and flourish in such an environment is if scientifically valid evaluations establish that it works—most likely through conventional measures such as student test scores and GPAs, but also through newly developed metrics that better measure whether students are acquiring the 4C skills that educators (and I) believe are essential for workplace and life success in the twenty-first century. That is why the next point is so important.

Third, given the huge demands on limited funds at all levels of government, there is no reasonable prospect that proper, scientifically rigorous evaluations of DCI tried (Chicago and Boston), let alone assessments of future rollouts of DCI in other places, will happen without philanthropic support. That is why I view professionals in that community—one to which I used to belong—as a prime audience for this book.

Fourth, even establishing that DCI works in the narrow sense of improving test scores, however imperfect these measures are, may not be enough to do the trick. That is because DCI is not only a pedagogical tool and suffers from the first challenge already outlined, but also because it may be viewed too narrowly. There may, and probably will, be a need to advance DCI as a part of a broader campaign for educational innovation and/or perhaps as a means for ensuring more equal educational opportunity. More about this soon.

In outlining my own thoughts for how to overcome these challenges to implementing DCI on a much larger scale than it has been used so far, I draw heavily on the excellent analysis of social change by Leslie Crutchfield. The subtitle of her latest book, *How Change Happens: Why Some Social Movements Succeed While Others Don't,* explains why her book is so important for those in the policymaking business.[2] Crutchfield is one of the country's leading experts on the dynamics of social change, writing and teaching from her perch as executive director of Georgetown University's Global Social Enterprise Initiative at the school's McDonough School of Business. Her conclusions are based on an exhaustive analysis of a team of social scientists she has led that have studied the keys to success for a variety of different social movements. Though I am calling for the widespread adoption of DCI as a teaching technique, I am not advocating a broad social movement, given the distinctive challenges just outlined. Even so, the lessons Crutchfield describes are still relevant to my suggestions.

The initiatives in Crutchfield's study include the anti-tobacco movement, efforts on behalf of the LGBTQ community that have made marriage equality the law of the land, successful efforts of gun rights advocates to block much of the gun control agenda over the past several decades, the movement behind toughening laws and enforcement against drunk driving, and the global eradication of polio. Despite their variety, Crutchfield finds that these movements shared several features in common. The following discussion examines these shared features and the implications they have for the diffusion of DCI in middle and high schools. Collectively, they offer a playbook of how to instill major social change, though in the case of DCI, there are some special twists.

Focus on Local and State Levels

Crutchfield's first lesson is that most big successful social movements start from the bottom—at the local and state levels—and eventually reach their way to Washington through legislation or judicial rulings, ultimately by the Supreme Court. This observation explains the success of each of the domestic initiatives or movements just listed, as well as why the efforts at gun control—at least so far—have been unsuccessful. The latter sought change only at the federal level, with very limited success, notably the Brady Bill that required federal background checks for gun purchases, with a five-day waiting period so the check could be completed. In every other case, including that of the pro-gun rights movement, the initiatives developed grassroots support and organized for changes at the local and state levels before any meaningful action was taken at the federal level.

This first lesson—build support at the state and local level before taking on Washington—is not directly applicable to education reform in the same way it has applied to the social movements surveyed in Crutchfield's study. That is because K–12 education has long been, and almost surely will remain, primarily a local and state responsibility. Nonetheless, the federal government is not irrelevant to educational policy, even though it provides only about 10 percent of all K–12 funding. Federal monies come with conditions for receiving those funds. In addition, the U.S. Department of Education supports evaluations of various reform initiatives adopted at the local and state levels. Still, if DCI is to be implemented more widely, it will have to occur in localities first, and that is why ground-level support for it must be generated.

Grass Roots Support and Networking

Related to a bottom-up strategy for driving successful change is the use of networks within and across cities and states, all working toward a common objective. In the case of education reform, especially pedagogical reform, this is difficult because our decentralized system encourages experimentation at the school and even teacher level, even as it insists on students being constantly measured by standardized tests. In other words, the result—higher test scores—may be widely agreed upon, though there are good reasons why this shouldn't be so. In any event, the methods of achieving those results, from "drill and kill" to the various unstructured classroom experiments highlighted in Ted Dintersmith's book, vary across schools, districts, and states.

In such an environment, even statistically valid proof that DCI works—judged by any number of metrics—is unlikely, by itself, to unify teachers, principals, or school boards to substantially increase the odds of widespread implementation. For a reform network to be formed that has sustained energy, a broader reform umbrella may be needed.

One such umbrella might be formed around an "Innovate the Classroom" agenda, one that would encourage school boards and superintendents to permit greater teacher autonomy in the classroom, though at least in the short run and until better measures of student performance are developed and widely agreed upon, schools still would be judged by overall test scores. However, because DCI is focused on engaging students in middle school, where the drop-off in student interest appears greatest, and also in high school where continued engagement is especially important, attendance and, ultimately, graduation rates should be almost as useful as test scores, maybe even more, as measures of success.

Under a Classroom Innovation agenda, school districts would do much more to expose teachers during their professional development time to an array of innovative pedagogical methods, including DCI. Teachers interested in gaining additional expertise in delivering DCI could do so over the summer in specialized institutes for initial cohorts, ideally funded by philanthropic dollars, using teachers who have been trained and have used the technique in classrooms to their satisfaction.

Linking DCI to a broader Classroom Innovation agenda would have the advantage of also connecting it to advocates of other successful pedagogical reform initiatives, such as project-based learning and EdLeaders21, now run by Battelle for Kids. The key to this networking strategy is to combine forces of those working in the trenches implementing various pedagogical reforms, and to do so in a way that does not promote one innovation over another. Indeed, one special attraction of DCI is that it develops communications, research, and critical thinking skills that are useful in all kinds of specialized school environments—such as STEM, the arts, entrepreneurship—and across virtually all school subjects. In this way, DCI can enhance the effectiveness of other innovation initiatives and should be positioned as such, not as a competitor, which it clearly is not.

Parents also can and should be engaged to support a Classroom Innovations agenda, especially parents with experience in competitive debate who would be likely backers of a DCI component of a broader Innovation movement. After all, parents have marched along with teachers when the latter have protested for increases in teacher salaries. Parents should be even more motivated to support teachers who are marching and organizing for better education for their kids!

Changing Minds and Hearts

Big social movements don't succeed without changing "hearts and minds," not just policies. People must be persuaded to think differently, and only then will behavior, private and public, change. Crutchfield explains how LGBTQ advocates changed the way homosexuals were (and too often still are) treated in our society. It helped that some brave individuals eventually felt safe enough to "come out of the closet," and when they did, millions of families across America realized they did not want their children or close relatives to be treated as they had in the past. She could have added that the civil rights movement eventually was successful because Martin Luther King confronted America with the stark contrast with the bold ideal of equal rights embodied in the Constitution and the reality on the ground that this was far from true for black Americans. Eventually, attitudes and the law changed—though as a nation we still have a way to go.

Changing minds and hearts is relevant to diffusing DCI. After all, a major rationale for DCI is that it should instill a mindset in students to be amenable to change their minds when the facts warrant. I am under no illusion that everyone exposed to DCI in school will react the same way, but the directional effect should be clear: toward more open-mindedness.

Of course, to have more schools and teachers use DCI in the classroom will require parents, teachers, and others in the educational establishment to be open-minded, as well. It is quite legitimate to ask whether citizens in our highly polarized country want their children to be open-minded when they grow up. Some may not. But I believe most parents want their children to learn how to learn, and to be able to adapt to the changes that the twenty-first century will impose on them whether they like it or not. That's all the open-mindedness that is required to support wider implementation of DCI in schools.

Break from "Business as Usual"

All successful social movements, by definition, forge a change in attitudes and policies. Accordingly, they represent a "break from business as usual," another one of the criteria Crutchfield discusses. Sometimes that break occurs because the idea behind the movement appeals to parties or interest groups that otherwise would be on opposite sides.

One example Crutchfield cites is the development in the late 1980s and implementation through the Clean Air Act Amendments of 1990 of caps on the emissions of sulfur dioxide, which produces acid rain (killing vegetation and fish and eroding structures) but allows permits for such emissions to be traded among SO_2 polluters. This "cap and trade" policy was remarkably successful, sharply reducing SO_2 emissions and eventually restoring fish to lakes where they had come close to extinction.

Cap and trade represented a sharp break from business as usual, both for environmental advocates and for the business community. Until the idea was pioneered for SO_2 management (and continues to be advocated as one way of curtailing carbon dioxide emissions responsible for climate change), pollution was limited solely through detailed "command and control" regulations backed up by lawsuits. Cap and trade harnesses the market to reduce pollution in a far more cost-effective way: by letting polluters decide whether it is cheaper to buy permits or to implement ways of reducing their emissions. This virtue convinced some key environmental groups—notably the Environmental Defense Fund, which largely designed the idea—to abandon their previous opposition to any policy that smacked of letting polluters' pay for pollution. At the same time, cap and trade persuaded many in the business community that this was a better way to reduce pollution than abiding by detailed rules and often litigating over their content or compliance with them (many economists have argued implementing a carbon tax is an even more cost-effective way to reduce pollution).

DCI also represents a break from business as usual in education—from the long-used lecture format, sometimes punctuated with Socratic dialogue from the teacher or unstructured classroom discussion—into a more structured but highly active method of learning concentrating on improving the critical thinking and oral communication skills of students. In principle, DCI should be welcomed by teachers, who would be under less pressure to lecture all the time and, instead, could act as mentors and facilitators during some portion of the week. Likewise, DCI should be welcomed by principals, superintendents, and school boards to the extent it works—enhancing students' educational performance and interest in learning.

Of course, despite the presumptive case I have made that DCI, indeed, does work and will improve not only educational but also workplace and civic outcomes, there is room for having more rigorous proof of all this. That is why the next factor I discuss in this chapter, not common to all the successful social movements surveyed by Crutchfield, is so important to the widespread implementation of DCI.

Philanthropic Support

Philanthropic support was useful to some successful social movements, perhaps no more so than in the case of anti-tobacco campaign. Crutchfield identifies the special roles played by the Robert Wood Johnson Foundation and the American Legacy Fund (created out of the monies from the settlement of anti-tobacco litigation).

Philanthropies have played a key role in educational reform efforts to date, as well. Leading funders have included, among many others, the Gates Foundation, best known for its major funding of smaller high schools; the Walton Family Foundation, for its support of public charter schools; Max Fisher, for his funding of the largest and one of the most effective charter school networks, the Knowledge is Power Program schools (KIPP); and the Eli and Edythe Broad Foundation, for its support of leadership training of superintendents in urban school districts.

Philanthropies have been important to the funding of education reform initiatives and also their evaluation. To its credit, Gates supported an independent evaluation of its teacher effectiveness initiative by the Rand Corporation, which reached generally disappointing conclusions.[3] Evaluations of KIPP and other "no excuses" charter schools like the Success Academy schools in New York, funded by foundations, have been much more positive. Foundations that have been especially active in education evaluations include the Arnold Foundation (which has been a leader in funding and advocating the importance of "evidence-based" policy) and the Smith Richardson Foundation (on whose domestic advisory board I was privileged to sit from 2013 through 2019).

The preceding chapters, taken together, warrant philanthropic support of both additional DCI experiments and their evaluation. There is strong presumptive evidence from the limited empirical evidence relating to the benefits of competitive debate, as well as the before-after results of DCI initiatives in public schools in Boston and Chicago. More formal, rigorous evaluations of these initiatives, however, will be required if the educational benefits of DCI are to be validated. Ideally, future evaluations would be sufficiently forward looking to examine whether DCI also delivers the citizenship and workplace benefits of DCI outlined in chapters 4 and 5. But even less ambitious evaluations of just the short-term educational benefits of DCI would be worthwhile.

Nonetheless, as I have argued, the presumptive evidence supporting the educational benefits of DCI is sufficiently strong that wider implementation of the technique is warranted. Ideally, philanthropic dollars will be there to support rigorous evaluations when and where that happens.

Handling Adversarial Allies

No movement for social change is homogeneous. Successful change is typically accomplished, in Crutchfield's analysis, through an alliance of multiple organizations, leaders, and grassroots supporters, all of whom agree on the objective—such as reducing tobacco use or drunk driving—but may differ on the best means to achieve it.

Crutchfield identifies intra-movement strife as an impediment to success. When leaders of different factions let their egos get in the way, or fight over who gets the credit, momentum for change can slow or come to a stop. Such fights need to be managed and defused. The following widely repeated quote from President Reagan says it all: "There is no limit to the amount of good you can do if you don't care who gets the credit."[4]

While validation from rigorous study is a prerequisite for wider adoption of DCI, it is not a sufficient condition, as the other elements for successful change identified by Crutchfield and surveyed in this chapter attest. This is especially true because, as noted at the outset of this chapter, DCI is a pedagogical tool, which may make it difficult to rally grassroots support, even if those grassroots are highly influential, respected school leaders, superintendents, and local board members.

Moreover, there are other pedagogical reforms out there that appear to be successful and advocates understandably want to scale the reform they know most about. For this reason, I suggested earlier that DCI be advocated as part of a larger Classroom Innovation agenda that includes other innovative classroom reforms. A larger reform tent need not threaten support of other initiatives aimed at improving education.

But allies can also introduce friction. Money raised and volunteer time committed for a wider Classroom Innovation initiative ideally would advance all the innovation ideas captured under the larger umbrella. Some firm believers in their own special innovation, however, may want special emphasis on that innovation at the expense of the others. Or the notion of the Innovation umbrella may be viewed as a threat to the wider adoption of specific innovations. These are the kind of intra-movement rivalries, even if there are no personal ego clashes between the leaders of the different innovation initiatives, that can doom the entire effort.

But if DCI alone is unlikely to be widely adopted outside of a broader reform initiative, then advocates of DCI, like me, will need to come up with a way to persuade other innovation leaders to join in a common effort, such as arguing that the success of each initiative will be more assured if all of them are linked together. Given the close relationship between DCI and project-based learning—the latter being a broader term that encompasses many innovations, including DCI—pressing more school districts and schools to adopt some form of PBL while mentioning that it covers DCI looks like the best way to do that.

Timing

So many people have said "timing is everything" that I couldn't find in an internet search who said it first. It doesn't matter, because it is true in all walks of life. Many good ideas and products never make it, because they were introduced too early, when conditions weren't ripe for their acceptance. The timing had to be right for the first African American to become president of the United States in 2008. Likewise, Donald Trump's timing was just right in pursuing his presidential candidacy in 2016. I am confident both men would admit that had they run in different years their campaigns wouldn't have been successful.

Debate and DCI are no different in this regard. So far, it has been overlooked as a way not only to improve education in America but to help us all get along. The polarization in America cries out for innovative ways of bringing the country back together. Although there are those on both sides of the political spectrum who do not want accommodation with the other side, team, or tribe, I believe most Americans want our society and government to work. As more attention is given to the virtues of evidence-based debate, an idea I hope this book will stimulate others to supplement and expand upon, dispirited Americans can have some hope that our civic discourse can eventually improve.

The timing for debate-centered education is right on the economic front, as well. With inequality rising and the ability to realize the American Dream fading, large numbers of Americans are desperate for constructive solutions, if not for themselves then at least for their children. The soft skills that debate provides also turn out to be important skills for the workforce, skills that can drive innovation and productivity, which are the keys to higher wages. The more Americans who have these skills—and let's start with our high school students who are not far from joining the labor force, even or especially if they go on to two- or four-year colleges—the more broadly shared higher incomes will be. This is good for our future workforce and for the health of our economy.

To be clear, I am not claiming that introducing DCI in nondebate courses will magically solve all the problems in our educational system, let alone conquer the political and economic problems of the country. As noted in chapter 1, former Education Secretary Arne Duncan argues powerfully in his book *How Schools Work* that major increases in teacher pay, coupled with true accountability and multiple measures for reducing gun violence in schools (not just reasonable gun control measures), stand at the top of any "to do" list to improve U.S. education, especially in its inner-city schools.

My claim, rather, is more modest: that much wider participation in debate and the introduction of DCI techniques also belong high on the education reform agenda, and that experiments with this idea, with the recognition that it has potentially important ancillary benefits, cannot begin soon enough. To wait until teachers are paid consistent with the value they add to our society, or even before more rigorous evaluations of the idea are in or before additional experiments with DCI are undertaken, is to sacrifice the benefits of a reform that can excite both students and teachers while eventually helping to heal our society and improve the flexibility and productivity of our future workforce.

Leadership

Finally, common to all the successful social movements profiled by Crutchfield is effective leadership, often but not necessarily by a charismatic individual. To be quite clear, I am not nominating myself to be the leader of a "DCI movement" among schools, for any number of reasons, the most prominent being that I have never taught a class in K–12, and at the time of publication of this book, I am seventy years old (I am shaking my head as I write the number you just read!).

Fortunately, there are individuals I have met and interacted with during the course of researching and writing this book who could be effective national leaders reaching out to philanthropies, the teacher community, and school leaders across the nation to make widespread use of DCI, adapted to the needs of particular types of students and classes and to the capabilities and inclinations of individual teachers. I will not name them to avoid putting them in an awkward position. I think they know who they are. But any or all the candidates I have in mind may decide that national organizing is not their strong suit, and that they would rather stick to refining and expanding what they are already doing.

I am confident, however, that if DCI spreads and future evaluations validate its effectiveness, and more teachers and potentially even students get exposed to and gain experience with DCI, future leaders of a DCI movement, alone or as part of a broader education innovation reform initiative, will emerge. It is with this thought and hope that I close this book, and it is to those individuals who will, in the future, take up the mantle of leadership and the rest of Americans who will benefit from it, that this book is devoted.

Notes

Preface

1. Crista Case Bryant, "Need Help Winning an Argument? Ask a Kansas High Schooler," *Christian Science Monitor*, April 11, 2018, www.csmonitor.com/EqualEd/2018/0411/Need-help-winning-an-argument-Ask-a-Kansas-high-schooler.

2. Robert E. Litan, "A Counterintuitive Proposal for Improving Education and Healing America: Debate-Centered Instruction." *Brown Center Chalkboard* (blog), Brookings Institution, September 27, 2018. www.brookings.edu/blog/brown-center-chalkboard/2018/09/27/a-counterintuitive-proposal-for-improving-education-and-healing-america-debate-centered-instruction.

Chapter 1

1. Quoted in Kevin Minch Kent Summers, eds., "Making the Case for Forensics," National Federation of State High School Associations (2006), www.speechanddebate.org/wp-content/uploads/Making-The-Case-NFHS.pdf.

2. The level of attachment that voters have for either party may not be as important as what voters on each side believe about those on the other—the

worst. Self-identified Democrats and Republicans strongly believe in caricatures of people in the rival political camp, and literally detest others for fitting these caricatures. See More in Common (website), "The Perception Gap," June 2019, https://perceptiongap.us/.

3. Mark Muro and Jacob Whiton, "America Has Two Economies—And They're Diverging Fast," Brooking Institution, September 19, 2019, www.brookings.edu/blog/the-avenue/2019/09/10/america-has-two-economies-and-theyre-diverging-fast/.

4. Levi Boxell, Matthew Gentzkow, Jesse M. Shapiro, "Cross-Country Trends in Affective Polarization," Stanford Institute for Economic Policy Research, Jan 2020 Working Paper, 20-004, at https://siepr.stanford.edu/research/publications/cross-country-trends-affective-polarization-0. The authors measured trends in polarization (negative attitudes toward those in other parties) in nine OECD countries over the past four decades, finding the U.S. experienced the largest increase in polarization over this period.

5. Jim Mattis, "Duty, Democracy and the Threat of Tribalism," *Wall Street Journal*, August 28, 2019.

6. See E. J. Dionne, Kayla Melzter Drogosz, Robert E. Litan, eds., *National Service and the Future of Citizenship* (Washington, D.C.: Brookings Institution, 2003). More recently, see Stanley A. McChrystal and Michael E. O'Hanlon, "How a Focus on National Service can Unify our Divided Country," Brookings Institution, March 5, 2019, www.brookings.edu/blog/order-from-chaos/2019/03/05/how-a-focus-on-national-service-can-unify-our-divided-country/.

7. See "No Debate About It," Broward County Public Schools Debate Initiative, 2017: www.browardschools.com/cms/lib/FL01803656/Centricity/Domain/13621/debate-brochure-2017.pdf

8. Based on interviews with Marjorie Stoneman's former debate coach Jesus Caro, July 30, 2018 and August 15, 2018.

9. See website for "Speak First," Impact America, at https://impactamerica.com/speakfirst/.

10. Information obtained in oral interview.

11. See the website: argumentcenterededucation.com.

12. See especially Joe Bellon, "A Research-Based Justification for Debate Across the Curriculum," *Argumentation and Advocacy* 36, Winter 2000, 161–75, https://millennialsd.com/wp-content/uploads/2014/03/bellon-debate-across-the-curriculum.pdf. Other authors who have made similar arguments in other publications are referenced in chapter 3.

13. Interview in October, 2018.

14. Lucy Crehan, *Clever Lands: The Secrets Behind the Success of the World's Education Superpowers* (London: Unbound, 2016), p. 200.

15. Readers interested in learning more about PBL can go to this website: pbworks.com.

16. Tom Vander Ark, "Getting Started with High School Redesign," March 21, 2019, atwww.linkedin.com/pulse/getting-started-high-school-redesign-tom-vander-ark/?published=t.

17. Jal Mehta and Sarah Fine, "High School Doesn't Have to Be Boring," *New York Times*, March 30, 2019.

18. Ibid.

19. Yuval Noah Harari, *21 Lessons for the 21st Century* (New York: Speigel & Grau, 2018), p. 222.

20. Peggy Noonan, "A Magic Pony is the Wrong Horse to Back," *Wall Street Journal*, December 15–16, 2018, p. A13.

21. Jason Riley, "The Blue Wave May Wash Education Reform Away," *Wall Street Journal*, November 14, 2018, p. A17.

22. Ben Lindbergh and Travis Sawchik, *The MVP Machine: How Baseball's New Nonconformists are Using Data to Build Better Players* (New York: Basic Books, 2019).

23. Arne Duncan, *How Schools Work* (New York: Simon & Schuster, 2018).

Chapter 2

1. Elvyn Jones, "Senior Brings National Champion Confidence to LHS Debate Squad," LJWorld.com, November 23, 2018, www2.ljworld.com/news/schools/2018/nov/23/senior-brings-national-champion-confidence-to-lhs-debate-squad/.

2. For a history of the NFL/NSDA, see www.speechanddebate.org/history/.

3. For a history and categorization of kritik arguments, see William Bennett, "An Introduction to the 'Kritik,'" https://debate.uvm.edu/NFL/rostrumlib/cxkbennett0496.pdf.

4. For examples of kritik arguments, see "What Is the 'Critique' or 'Kritik'"? Powerpoint presentation, 2016, www.nfhs.org/media/1017640/introduction-to-kritiks-2016.pdf.

5. Joe Miller, *Cross-X: The Amazing True Story of How the Most Unlikely Team from the Most Unlikely of Places Overcame Staggering Obstacles at Home and at School to Challenge . . . Community on Race, Power, and Education* (New York: Farrar, Straus and Giroux, 2007).

6. See www.debatecoaches.org/resources/open-evidence-project/.

7. Jonathan Ellis and Francesca Hovagimian, "Are School Debate Competitions Bad for Our Political Discourse?" *New York Times*, October 13, 2019.

8. I thank Les Lynn for making this point to me.

9. Lee Bell, "IBM's Project Debater Loses to Human Champ in Live

Showdown," The Inquirer, February 12, 2019, www.theinquirer.net/inquirer/news/3070860/ibm-project-debater-loses-to-human.

10. See also Cade Metz and Steve Lohr, "IBM Unveils System that 'Debates' with Humans," June 21, 2018, www.nytimes.com/2018/06/18/technology/ibm-debater-artificial-intelligence.html.

11. For an excellent discussion of the leading example—supply-side tax cuts that had little or no evidence backing them, either before or after they were implemented—see Alan S. Blinder, *Advice and Dissent* (New York: Basic Books, 2018).

12. This book is the best introduction to this subject that I have seen, and certainly the most entertaining. See Andrew Leigh, *Randomistas: How Radical Researchers are Changing the World* (Yale University Press, 2018).

13. Briana Mezuk, Irina Bondarenk, Suzanne Smith and Eric Tucker, "Impact of Participating in a Policy Debate Program on Academic Achievement: Evidence from the Chicago Urban Debate League," *Educational Research and Reviews* 6, no. 9 (September 5, 2011), 622–35.

14. Ibid, p. 622.

15. Susannah Anderson and Briana Mezuk, "Positive Youth Development and Participation in an Urban Debate League: Results from Chicago Public Schools," *The Journal of Negro Education* 84, no. 3 (summer 2015), 362–78.

16. Daniel T. Shackelford, Scott M. Ratliff, and Briana Mezuk, "Participating in a High School Debate Program and College Matriculation and Completion: Evidence from the Chicago Debate League," *Educational Research and Reviews* 4, no. 11 (June 10, 2019), 397–409.

17. Daniel Shackelford, "The BUDL Effect: Modeling Academic Achievement and Engagement Outcomes of Preadolescent Baltimore Urban Debate League Participants," *Educational Researcher* 48, no. 3 (February 26, 2019), 145–57.

Chapter 3

1. National Commission on Excellence in Education, *A Nation at Risk: The Imperative for Educational Reform A Report to the Nation and the Secretary of Education United States Department of Education*, April 1983.

2. Institute of Education Sciences, What Works Clearinghouse (webpage), https://ies.ed.gov/ncee/wwc/.

3. National Center for Education Statistics, *The Nation's Report Card: Trends in Academic Progress*, U.S. Department of Education, June 2013, https://nces.ed.gov/nationsreportcard/subject/publications/main2012/pdf/2013456.pdf.

4. Ashraf Khalil, Jeff Amy, and Carolyn Thompson, "American Students' Performance Lags on Nation's Report Card," Associated Press, October 30, 2019, https://apnews.com/565be54d26354e72b02a813593923fef?utm_source=newsletter&utm_medium=email&utm_campaign=newsletter_axiosam&stream=top.

5. Louis Serino, "What International Test Scores Reveal about American Education," *Brown Center Chalkboard* (blog), Brookings Institution, April 7, 2017, www.brookings.edu/blog/brown-center-chalkboard/2017/04/07/what-international-test-scores-reveal-about-american-education/.

6. Kim Parker, Rich Morin, and Juliana Menasce Horwowitz, "Looking to the Future, Public Sees an America in Decline on Many Fronts, Pew Research Center, March 21, 2019, www.pewsocialtrends.org/2019/03/21/public-sees-an-america-in-decline-on-many-fronts; Serino, "What International Test Scores Reveal."

7. Lena V. Groeger, Annie Waldman, and David Eads, "Miseducation": Is There Racial Inequality at Your School? ProPublica, October 16, 2018, https://projects.propublica.org/miseducation. This website allows readers to explore racial disparities all across the United States.

8. Greg Lukianoff and Jonathan Haidt, *The Coddling of the American Mind: How Good Intentions and Bad Ideas Are Setting Up a Generation for Failure* (New York: Penguin Press, 2018).

9. Sheryl Sandberg, *Lean In: Women, Work, and the Will to Lead* (New York: Knopf, 2013).

10. This brief history Is drawn from Allie Bidwell, "The History of Common Core Standards," *US News and World Report*, February 27, 2014, www.usnews.com/news/special-reports/articles/2014/02/27/the-history-of-common-core-state-standards.

11. See "Map: Tracking the Common Core State Standards," Education Week, June 29, 2015, www.edweek.org/ew/section/multimedia/map-states-academic-standards-common-core-or.html.

12. Chapter 3 of the *Official SAT Study Guide* states: "Your [students'] command of evidence will be tested throughout much of the SAT, including the Reading Test, the Writing and Language Test, and the optional Essay."

13. *Common Core State Standards for English Language Arts & Literacy in History/Social Studies, Science, and Technical Subjects Appendix A: Research Supporting Key Elements of the Standards,* p. 24, www.corestandards.org/assets/Appendix_A.pdf.

14. National Education Assocation, "Preparing 21st Century Students for a Global Society: An Educator's Guide to the 4Cs," www.nea.org/assets/docs/A-Guide-to-Four-Cs.pdf.

15. Ancient History Encyclopedia (website), "Protagoras," www.ancient.eu/protagoras.

16. R. A. Mercadante, "Formal Debate as a Pedagogical Tool in the College Classroom," paper presented at the National Seminar on Successful College Teaching, Orlando, Florida, March 1988, https://files.eric.ed.gov/fulltext/ED384943.pdf; Thomas Lee Budesheim and Arlene R. Lundquist, "Consider the Opposite: Opening Minds through In-Class Debates on Course-Related Controversies," *Teaching of Psychology* 26, no. 2, 106–10.

17. Joe Bellon, "A Research-Based Justification for Debate Across the Curriculum," *Argumentation and Advocacy* 36, no. 3 (Winter 2000), pp. 161–75.

18. Taylor Lorenz, "Where Teens Are Debating News on Instagram," *The Atlantic*, July 26, 2018, www.theatlantic.com/technology/archive/2018/07/the-instagram-forums-where-teens-go-to-debate-big-issues/566153/.

19. Budesheim and Lundquist confirmed this in their limited experiment with requiring students to take both sides in three classroom settings. It also is just common sense.

20. Dara Hensley and Diana Carlin, *Mastering Competitive Debate*, 8th edition (Clark Publishing Company, 2020).

21. Lynn points to Gerald Graff, Cathy Birkenstein, Deanna Kuhn, and David Zarefsky, all experts, among others, in rhetoric and argumentation and all of whom are listed on the "Debatifier" feature of his website, argument-centerededucation.com. Wasserman and several teachers coached by the BDL singled out Katherine McNeill, who has written extensively on how to apply the "claims-evidence-reasoning" methodology in teaching the sciences.

22. Ted Dintersmith, *What School Could Be* (Princeton University Press, 2018); PBLworks.org.

23. See the website: argumentcenterededucation.com/.

24. Les Lynn, "Dismantling Racially-Motivated Arguments for Exclusion," Argument-Centered Education, August 4, 2018, http://argumentcenterededucation.com/2018/08/04/dismantling-racially-motivated-arguments-for-exclusion/.

25. Adam Grant, "Kids, Would You Please Start Fighting?" *New York Times*, November 4, 2017, www.nytimes.com/2017/11/04/opinion/sunday/kids-would-you-please-start-fighting.html.

26. See "The Exeter Difference" (webpage), Phillips Exeter Academy, www.exeter.edu/exeter-difference/how-youll-learn; and "Harkness" (webpage), The Lawrenceville School, www.lawrenceville.org/page/academics/harkness.

27. Abdullah provided this information in an interview with the author during a visit to the school on April 26, 2019.

28. Jay Heinrichs, *Thank You for Arguing* 2nd edition (New York: Three Rivers Press, 2013), p. 37.

29. For a video explaining the program, see "Why The Art of Speaking Should Be Taught Alongside Math and Literacy," Mindshift, October 3, 2016, www.kqed.org/mindshift/46546/why-the-art-of-speaking-should-be-taught-alongside-math-and-literacy?fbclid=IwAR1J7eScLXYAIA-T-sr5-OTjtaGCGsgD ALQF6Zpa3nufTwhoJLH7C9H_6-k.

30. I found this quote courtesy of Van Jones, who puts this Franklin quote prominently in his book *Beyond the Messy Truth: How We Came Apart, How We Come Together* (Ballentine Books, 2017). It is available at www.brainyquote. com/quotes/benjamin_franklin_383997.

31. Dintersmith, *What School Could Be* (2018), pp. 178–79.

32. As concluded in *The Economist,* "Young Americans: Republicans and Democrats Are Taking Early Education More Seriously," January 26, 2019: "All the evidence suggests that children from poorer backgrounds are at a disadvantage almost as soon as they are born. By the age of five or six they are far less 'school ready' than their better-off peers . . ."

33. In the same issue of *The Economist,* the childhood survey notes that the rapid expansion of pre-K programs using low-paid staff with high turnover rates may yield disappointing results, citing that "earnings are so paltry that 58% of child-care workers in California qualify for some form of public assistance."

34. Alan Blinder, *Advice and Dissent: Why America Suffers When Economics and Politics Collide* (New York: Basic Books, 2018), p. 219.

35. See, for example, Robert H. Dugger and Robert E. Litan, *Early Childhood 'Pay-For-Success' Social Impact Finance: A PKSE Bond Example to Increase School Readiness and Reduce Special Education Costs,* a report from the Kaufmann Foundation and ReadyNation, Working Group on Early Childhood Finance Innovation, March 2012, http://humcap.uchicago.edu/RePEc/hka/wpaper/ Dugger_Litan_2012_early-childhood-pay.pdf.

36. For a good summary of the evidence, see "Special Report: Childhood," *The Economist,* January 5, 2019, http://weblogibc-co.com/wp-content/uploads /2019/01/The-Economist-2019-01-05.pdf.

37. Dintersmith, *What School Could Be* (2018).

38. Angela Duckworth, *Grit: The Power of Passion and Perseverance* (New York: Scribner, 2016).

39. Based on materials provided by Lynn to the author.

40. Based on materials provided by Wasserman to the author.

41. Twitter post by Norman Ornstein, March 13, 2019.

42. Ian Prasad Philbrick, "What These Debaters Learned from the 2020 Democratic Presidential Debates," *New York Times*, August 4, 2019.

43. Lukianoff and Haidt, *The Coddling of the American Mind* (2018), p. 248.

44. Mercadante, "Formal Debate as a Pedagogical Tool in the College Classroom (1988).

45. Ruth Kennedy, "In-Class Debates: Fertile Ground for Active Learning and the Cultivation of Critical Thinking and Oral Communication Skills," *International Journal of Teaching and Learning in Higher Education* 19, no. 2 (2007), 183–90.

46. Since the list changes, try typing into any internet search engine "debate in college instruction."

47. Dintersmith, *What School Could Be* (1988), pp. 93–94.

48. Pezhman Zare and Moomala Othman, "Students' Perceptions toward Using Classroom Debate to Develop Critical Thinking and Oral Communication Ability," *Asian Social Science* 11, no. 9 (2015), https://pdfs. semanticscholar.org/bdf9/0ef78a76c9eef3f261873702ffofde5fbc1e.pdf.

49. Jean Goodwin, "Students' Perspectives on Debate Exercises in Content Area Classes," *Communication Education* 52, no. 2, 2003, 157–63.

50. Maria Y. Omelicheva, "Resolved: Academic Debate Should Be a Part of Political Science Curricula," *Journal of Political Science Education* 3 (2007), 161–75, www.semanticscholar.org/paper/Resolved%3A-Academic-Debate-Should-Be-a-Part-of-Omelicheva/e17261147838d586962b98f4a90493ae837ad469.

51. Sophia Scott, "Perceptions of Students' Learning Critical Thinking through Debate in a Technology Classroom: A Case Study," *Journal of Technology Studies* 34, no. 1 (2008), 39–44.

52. Howard W. Combs, et al., "The Renaissance of Educational Debate: Results of a Five-Year Study of the Use of Debate in Business Education," *Journal on Excellence in College Teaching* 5, no. 1 (1994), 57–67.

53. Owen Doody and M. Condon, "Increasing Student Involvement and Learning through Using Debate as an Assessment," *Nurse Education in Practice* 12 (2012), 232–37.

54. See Chein-Hui Yang and Enniati Rusli, "Using Debate as a Pedagogical Tool in Enhancing Pre-Service Teachers' Learning and Critical Thinking," *Journal of International Education Research* 2, no. 8 (2012), 135–44.

55. Kari Paul, Women Speak Up Less in College Seminars—Here's Why that Matters," MarketWatch, September 29, 2018, www.marketwatch.com/story/women-speak-up-less-in-academic-settings-heres-why-that-matters-2018-09-28.

56. Brenda Goodman, "Testosterone May Delay Boys' Speech Development,"

WebMD, January 26, 2012, www.webmd.com/parenting/baby/news/20120125/testosterone-may-delay-boys-speech-development#1.

57. "Debating Contests Teach Chinese Students an Argument Has Two Sides," *The Economist*, June 15, 2019, www.economist.com/china/2019/06/15/debating-contests-teach-chinese-students-an-argument-has-two-sides?fsrc=scn/tw/te/bl/ed/debatingconteststeachchinesestudentsanargumenthastwosidesoutofthestraitjacket.

Chapter 4

1. Christopher Walsh, "We Have a Civility Problem: Let's Fix It," George W. Bush Presidential Center, December 14, 2018, www.bushcenter.org/publications/articles/2018/12/civility-problem.html.

2. "When the Facts Change, I Change My Mind. What Do You Do, Sir?" Quote Investigator, https://quoteinvestigator.com/2011/07/22/keynes-change-mind/. A variation of this quote is widely attributed to British economist John Maynard Keynes, but it is not clear he ever said it.

3. Sandra L. Colby and Jennifer M. Ortman, "Projections of the Size and Composition of the U.S. Population, 2014–60," U.S. Census Bureau, March 2015, www.census.gov/content/dam/Census/library/publications/2015/demo/p25-1143.pdf.

4. The definitions here are offered from the *Oxford English Dictionary*.

5. Van Jones, *Beyond the Messy Truth: How We Came Apart, How We Come Together* (New York: Ballentine Books, 2017). The quote appears in a list of Jones's quotes on the Goodreads website: www.goodreads.com/author/quotes/472466.Van_Jones.

6. See "Frank H. Knight on Democracy as Discussion," November 14, 2011, https://vimeo.com/32101136. The video was created for presentation at a session on Democracy at the Chicago School of Economics for a Southern Economic Association meeting.

7. Peter H. Schuck, *One Nation Undecided: Clear Thinking about Five Hard Issues that Divide Us* (Princeton University Press, 2017).

8. For a fascinating look at how new technologies will pose new challenges for applying constitutional law, see Jeffrey Rosen and Benjamin Wittes, eds., *Constitution 3.0: Freedom and Technological Change* (Brookings Institution Press, 2011).

9. "The Twilight of Syriza," *The Economist,* March 23, 2019, p. 44.

10. Jill Lepore, *These Truths: A History of the United States* (New York. W.W. Norton, 2018), p. 116.

11. Quoted in Lepore, *These Truths* (2018), p. 146.

12. For an online version of the text of *The Federalist Papers*, see www. congress.gov/resources/display/content/The+Federalist+Papers.

13. Nancy Isenberg and Andrew Burstein, *The Problem of Democracy: The Presidents Adams Confront the Cult of Personality* (New York: Viking, 2019).

14. Gordon S. Wood, *The Idea of America: Reflections on the Birth of the United States* (New York: Penguin Books, 2011), p. 245.

15. Michael Tomasky, *If We Can Keep It: How the Republic Collapsed and How It Might be Saved* (New York: Liveright, 2019).

16. Levi Boxell, Matthew Gentzkow, Jesse M. Shapiro, "Cross-Country Trends in Affective Polarization, January 2020, www.brown.edu/Research/Shapiro/pdfs/cross-polar.pdf.

17. Jonathan Haidt, *The Righteous Mind: Why Good People Are Divided by Politics and Religion* (New York: Vintage, 2013).

18. Greg Lukianoff and Jonathan Haidt, *The Coddling of the American Mind: How Good Intentions and Bad Ideas Are Setting Up a Generation for Failure* (New York: Penguin, 2018), pp. 58–59.

19. Jon Meacham, "Mueller Offers a Lesson in the Power of Reason," *Time*, April 8, 2019, p. 28.

20. Roger McNamee, *Zucked* (New York: Penguin Press, 2019), p. 93.

21. On the importance of trust to economies and societies, see Francis Fukuyama, *Trust: Human Nature and the Reconstitution of Order* (New York: Free Press, 2008).

22. Daniel Kahneman, *Thinking Fast and Slow* (Princeton University Press, 2011), pp. 90–91.

23. Jonathan Haidt, *The Righteous Mind* (2012), pp. 152–53.

24. Richard E. Nisbett, *Mindware: Tools for Smart Thinking* (New York: Farrar, Straus and Giroux, 2015).

25. Daniel Kahneman, *Thinking Fast and Slow* (New York: Farrar, Straus and Giroux, 2011), p. 87.

26. Quote available on the Goodreads website: www.goodreads.com/quotes/4794-it-is-unwise-to-be-too-sure-of-one-s-own.

27. David Brooks, "An Era Defined by Fear," *New York Times*, April 30, 2019.

28. Quoted in Charles Duhigg, "Why Are We So Angry?" *The Atlantic*, January/February 2019, p. 71.

29. Darrell West, *Divided Politics Divided Nation* (Brookings Institution Press, 2019), p. 182.

30. Quote found at www.mindfueldaily.com/livewell/walking-a-mile-in-their-shoes-great-quotes-on-empathy/.

31. Sarah Ryan, "Arguing Toward a More Active Citizenry: Re-Envisioning

the Introductory Civics Course via Debate-Centered Pedagogy," *Journal of Public Affairs Education* 12, no. 3 (2006), pp. 385–95.

32. For an excellent guide to how Democratic presidential candidates are prepared for their debates, see Abby Witt, "How to Win Your Debate," Arena, October 22, 2018, https://arena.run/blog/how-to-win-your-debate.

33. Ben Yagoda, "The Cognitive Biases Tricking Your Brain," *The Atlantic*, August 4, 2018, www.theatlantic.com/feed/author/ben-yagoda/.

34. Morris P. Fiorina, *Unstable Majorities: Polarization, Party Sorting, and Political Stalemate* (Stanford, CA: Hoover Institution Press, 2017).

35. Ruy Teixeira, "The Great Illusion," *New Republic*, March 7, 2012, www.tnr.com/book/review/swing-vote-untapped-power-independents-linda-killian.

36. Jon Meacham, *The Soul of America* (New York: Random House, 2019), p. 29.

37. The ideas that follow are drawn from "We the People Are Bad at This," *Bloomberg Businessweek,* April 15, 2019, pp. 38–39.

38. In ranked voting, if no candidate wins a majority in the first round of voting, then the candidate with the fewest votes is dropped and his or her votes are reallocated to the remaining candidates according to those voters' second choices. This process continues until there is a "winner." For a thorough discussion of the potential benefits of ranked voting, see Lee Drutman, *Breaking the Two-Party Doom Loop: The Case for Multiparty Democracy in America* (Oxford University Press, 2020).

39. Jake Lefferman and Pavni Mittal, "Better Angels Group Puts Democrats and Republicans, Trump Supporters and Immigrants, in the Same Room to Listen to Each Other," ABC News, July 25, 2018. See the video that accompanies this report as one illustration of many: https://abcnews.go.com/Politics/angels-group-puts-democrats-republicans-trump-supporters-immigrants/story?id=56814771. For information about Better Angels, go to its website: www.better-angels.org/.

Chapter 5

1. For three broad overviews of why entrepreneurship is important for all economies, see William Baumol, Robert E. Litan, and Carl Schramm, *Good Capitalism, Bad Capitalism, and the Economics of Growth and Prosperity* (Yale University Press, 2007); Robert E. Litan and Carl Schramm, *Better Capitalism: Renewing the Entrepreneurial Strength of the American Economy* (Yale University Press, 2012); and William Baumol, *The Micro-Theory of Innovative Entrepreneurship* (Princeton University Press, 2010).

2. See, for example, Ian Hathaway and Robert E. Litan, "Declining Business Dynamism: It's for Real," Brookings Institution, May 22, 2014, https://www.brookings.edu/research/declining-business-dynamism-its-for-real/; and Ryan A. Decker, John Haltiwanger, Ron S. Jarman, and Javier Miranda, "Declining Business Dynamism: Implications for Productivity?" Brookings Institution, September 19, 2016, https://www.brookings.edu/research/declining-business-dynamism-implications-for-productivity/.

3. Amar Bhide, *The Venturesome Economy: How Innovation Sustains Prosperity in a More Connected World* (Princeton University Press, 2009).

4. Ian Hathaway and Robert E. Litan, "The Other Aging of America: The Increasing Dominance of Older Firms," Brookings Institution, July 31, 2014, https://www.brookings.edu/research/the-other-aging-of-america-the-increasing-dominance-of-older-firms/.

5. Quoted in Polina Marinova, "Kleiner Perkins: A Fallen Empire," *Fortune*, May 1, 2019, p. 93.

6. David Zarefsky, "What Does an Argument Culture Look Like," in *Rhetorical Perspectives on Argumentation*, January 2009, pp. 296–308.

7. Ray Dalio, *Principles: Life and Work* (New York: Simon & Schuster, 2017), p. 413.

8. Nina Zdinjak, "Bridgewater Associates' Returns, AUM, and Holdings," Yahoo Finance, November 16, 2018, finance.yahoo.com/news/bridgewater-associates-returns-aum-holdings-174743874.html.

9. Hal Gregersen, "The Secret to Asking Better Questions," *Wall Street Journal*, May 9, 2019, https://www.wsj.com/articles/to-be-a-better-leader-ask-better-questions-11557426294.

10. Robert Bruce Shaw, *Extreme Teams: Why Pixar, Netflix, Airbnb and Other Cutting-Edge Companies Succeed Where Most Fail* (American Management Association, 2019).

11. Ibid., p. 26.

12. Quoted in Laura Vanderkam, "One Target for Smart Giving," *Wall Street Journal*, April 22, 2019 (review of book by Melinda Gates, *The Moment of Lift*).

13. See, generally, Walter Isaacson, *Steve Jobs* (New York: Simon & Schuster, 2011).

14. Austin Carr and Dina Bass, "The Nadellaissance," *Bloomberg Businessweek*, May 6, 2019, pp. 38–41.

15. Julie Bort, "5 Best Things and 5 Worst Things about Working at Microsoft," Business Insider, June 26, 2016, www.inc.com/business-insider/5-best-worst-things-employees-working-microsoft-ceo-nadella.html. See also "Send in the Clouds," *The Economist*, July 6, 2019, p. 51.

16. Susie Gharib, "Novartis CEO: It's Time to "Pivot Towards Transformational Innovation," Fortune, March 20, 2019, http://fortune.com/2019/03/20/novartis-ceo-vasant-narasimhan-on-leading/?utm_source=fortune.com&utm_medium=email&utm_campaign=ceo-daily&utm_content=2019040911am.

17. Ibid.

18. Lauren Weber and Chip Cutter, "Class of 2019: Into the Fray," *Wall Street Journal*, May 11–12, 2019.

19. D. Deming, "The Growing Importance of Social Skills in the Labor Market," *Quarterly Journal of Economics* 132, no. 4 (2017), pp. 1593–1640.

20. GMAC Research Team, "Employers Seek Communication Skills in New Hires," MBA.com, January 1, 2018, www.mba.com/mbas-and-business-masters/articles/your-career-path/employers-seek-communications-skills.

21. Many economists have made these points. For my own contribution, see Robert E. Litan, "Meeting the Automation Challenge to the Middle Class and the American Project," Brookings Institution, June 21, 2018, https://www.brookings.edu/research/meeting-the-automation-challenge-to-the-middle-class-and-the-american-project/.

22. Aaron Smith and Monica Anderson, "Automation in Everyday Life," Pew Research Center, October 4, 2017, www.pewinternet.org/2017/10/04/automation-in-everyday-life/.

23. See especially Tyler Cowen, *Average Is Over: Powering America Beyond the Age of the Great Stagnation* (New York: Dutton, 2014).

24. Harry J. Holzer, "The Robots Are Coming. Let's Help the Middle Class Get Ready," *Up Front* (blog), Brookings Institution, December 13, 2018, www.brookings.edu/blog/up-front/2018/12/13/the-robots-are-coming-lets-help-the-middle-class-get-ready/.

25. Edward P. Lazear, "Mind the Productivity Gap to Reduce Inequality," *Wall Street Journal*, May 7, 2019, p. A17.

26. Heather Boushey, "The Economy Isn't Getting Better for Most Americans. But There Is A Fix," Op-Ed, Brookings Institution, May 15, 2019, www.brookings.edu/opinions/the-economy-isnt-getting-better-for-most-americans-but-there-is-a-fix/

27. See McKinsey & Company, *The Future of Work in America: People and Places, Today and Tomorrow*, July 2019, www.mckinsey.com/featured-insights/future-of-work/the-future-of-work-in-america-people-and-places-today-and-tomorrow.

28. See, for example, McKinsey & Company and Darrell West, *The Future of Work: Robots, AI, and Automation* (Washington, D.C.: Brookings Institution

Press, 2019); and Edward Alden and Laura Taylor-Kale, *The Work Ahead: Machines, Skills, and U.S. Leadership in the Twenty-First Century*, Council on Foreign Relations, Report of Independent Task Force #76, April 2018, www.cfr.org/report/the-work-ahead/report/.

29. I have coauthored books or articles advocating wage insurance since the mid-1980s with Brookings scholars Martin Baily, Lael Brainerd, Gary Burtless, and Robert Lawrence, as well as with non-Brookings researchers Lori Kletzer and Robert Shapiro.

30. Nick Hanauer, "Better Schools Won't Fix America," *The Atlantic*, July 2019, pp. 19–22.

31. John Lanchester, "Leveling the Playing Field," *Time*, February 4–11, 2019, p. 76.

32. Sarah Harrison, "AI May Not Kill Your Job—Just Change It," Wired, October 31, 2019, www.wired.com/story/ai-not-kill-job-change-it/.

33. Viktoryia Alexandrovna Kalesnikava, Gregory Paul Ekey, Tomohiro M. Ko, Daniel T. Shackelford, and Briana Mezuk, "Grit, Growth Mindset and Participation in Competitive Policy Debate: Evidence from the Chicago Debate League," *Educational Research and Reviews* 14, no. 10 (May 23, 2019), pp. 358–71.

34. Brooks tells his life story in Arthur C. Brooks, "Your Professional Decline Is Coming (Much) Sooner Than You Think," *The Atlantic*, June 2019, https://www.theatlantic.com/magazine/archive/2019/07/work-peak-professional-decline/590650/.

35. All information about Carroll's remarkable life story is drawn from Molly Petrilla, "Running the Show," *Pennsylvania Gazette*, July/August 2019, pp. 41–45.

Chapter 6

1. John F. Pfaff, *Locked In: The True Causes of Mass Incarceration and How to Achieve Real Reform* (New York, Basic Books, 2017).

2. Heather Van Benthuysen and Erica Hodgin, "Move Over Debate, It's Time to Deliberate," Teaching Channel, December 13, 2018, www.teachingchannel.org/tch/blog/move-over-debate-its-time-deliberate.

3. Trish Hall, *Writing to Persuade* (New York: W. W. Norton, 2019), pp. 103–07.

4. For a similar story about how ESL students can benefit from debate, see Vicky Papadopoulou, "Bring It On: 7 Questions Every ESL Teacher Has About Classroom Debates," *FluentU English Educator* (blog), www.fluentu.com/blog/educator-english/esl-debates/.

5. Amity Shlaes, "How to Bring Your Zombie Child to Life," *National*

Review, July 2014, www.nationalreview.com/2014/07/how-bring-your-zombie-child-life-amity-shlaes/.

6. The series is available at www.skiffmountainfilms.com/.

7. Samantha Schmidt, "How Maximum Security Inmates Took on Cambridge in a Debate about Nuclear Weapons—and Won," *Washington Post*, April 20, 2019, www.washingtonpost.com/local/social-issues/how-maximum-security-inmates-took-on-cambridge-in-a-debate-about-nuclear-weapons--and-won/2019/04/20/b333555e-609c-11e9-bfad-36a7eb36cb60_story.html.

8. Available on the Goodreads website: www.goodreads.com/quotes/63402-you-are-entitled-to-your-opinion-but-you-are-not.

9. Jonathan Rauch, "Fact-Checking the President in Real Time" *The Atlantic*, June 2019, pp. 11–14.

10. Drew Harwell, "Top AI Researchers Race to Detect 'Deepfake' Videos: 'We are Outgunned,'" *Washington Post,* June 12, 2019, www.washingtonpost.com/technology/2019/06/12/top-ai-researchers-race-detect-deepfake-videos-we-are-outgunned/?utm_term=.2a41c6ede319&wpisrc=nl_most&wpmm=1.

11. Rauch, "Fact-Checking the President in Real Time" (2019).

12. Lyndsey Layton, "Billions of Dollars on Annual Teacher Training Largely a Waste," *Washington Post*, August 4, 2015, www.washingtonpost.com/local/education/study-billions-of-dollars-in-annual-teacher-training-is-largely-a-waste/2015/08/03/c4e1f322-39ff-11e5-9c2d-ed991d848c48_story.html?utm_term=.f3d9a480b23d.

13. See http://argumentcenterededucation.com.

Chapter 7

1. Alan S. Blinder, *Advice and Dissent: Why America Suffers When Economics and Politics Collide* (New York: Basic Books, 2018).

2. Leslie R. Crutchfield. *How Change Happens: Why Some Social Movements Succeed While Others Don't* (Hoboken, New Jersey: John Wiley & Sons, 2018).

3. Madeline Will, "An Expensive Experiment': Gates Teacher-Effectiveness Program Shows No Gains for Students," June 21, 2018, Education Week, www.edweek.org/ew/articles/2018/06/21/an-expensive-experiment-gates-teacher-effectiveness-program-show.html.

4. Available on the Goodreads website: www.goodreads.com/quotes/29359-there-is-no-limit-to-the-amount-of-good-you.

Index